PRAISE FOR *MAKE HEALTHCARE WORK FOR YOU*

"Health and well-being are very personal and individualized; however, we throw employees into a very impersonal healthcare system with misaligned incentives. Darrell provides concrete examples on how to change this for the benefit of the individual and the company providing benefits."

K. Andrew Crighton, M.D., CPE, former retired Chief Medical Officer, Prudential Financial (1999-2019)

"*Make Healthcare Work for You* is packed with information to empower employers and patients to take charge of their healthcare to save money, improve access, and achieve better healthcare outcomes."

Dr. Ronke Komolafe, DBH, MBA, CEO Advancing Integrated Health, Founder of *Integrated Health Magazine*

"Darrell Moon has brought dedicated teams together to put the patient—the *person*—back in the center of healthcare. Together, we can bring *caring* back into healthcare. *You*, CEO, have the power, and Darrell can show you and help you to claim it. You have an army behind you, and the army is growing!"

Kimberlee Langford, BSN, R.N., CCM, CRMT, CPC, Vice President of Clinical Services for Specialty Care Management

"Darrell shares valuable insights for CEOs to transform both the health and healthcare of this country."

Betsy Foster, Co-Founder and President of Love.Life

"*Make Healthcare Work for You* empowers CEOs with information to leverage healthcare as a strategy to achieve a CEO's business objectives, rather than simply being a 'get it and forget it' purchase. In my opinion as a healthcare insider of over 30 years, the vision Darrell outlines in his book is a model of healthcare that will become a movement that sweeps through America in the coming years."

Bob Hilke, United Health Group (1988-2019), held various director-level positions including Director of Healthcare Operations, Operations Controller, Finance, Appeals, Communications, and Technology

MAKE HEALTHCARE WORK FOR YOU

HOW CEOS CAN TRANSFORM EMPLOYEE BENEFITS AND REDUCE MEDICAL SPENDING WITH ASPIRATIONAL HEALTHCARE

DARRELL T. MOON

Make Healthcare Work for You
How CEOs Can Transform Employee Benefits and Reduce Medical Spending With Aspirational Healthcare
Darrell T. Moon © 2024

Hardcover ISBN: 978-1-61206-329-4
Softcover ISBN: 978-1-61206-330-0
eBook ISBN: 978-1-61206-331-7

For more information about aspirational healthcare, visit Orriant.com

To purchase this book at quantity discounts, contact Aloha Publishing at alohapublishing@gmail.com

Published by

aloha PUBLISHING
AlohaPublishing.com

Printed in the United States of America

This book is dedicated to all the people who have committed their careers to transforming the U.S. healthcare system from being a financial machine to focusing on the health and well-being of the patient.

A special dedication to the Alaska Native and American Indian communities who have pioneered one of the best healthcare systems in the world, Southcentral Foundation's Nuka System of Care, setting an example of how healthcare should be built—for the customer.

CONTENTS

FOREWORD

Over the multiple decades of Darrell Moon's career, I have been both an observer and participant in his efforts to transform healthcare. Darrell holds a unique perspective, having held various C-suite leadership roles within the healthcare ecosystem. Taking that knowledge, Darrell continues to build important support solutions for group healthcare purchasers (employers) to better understand and navigate the challenges.

I commend Darrell's efforts through the aspirational healthcare model to demonstrate to CEOs that collaboration between healthcare providers and healthcare purchasers is required to rebuild the backbone of individual health in the U.S.

I have often said Darrell is the "little engine that could." Darrell's commitment to prevention, wellness, chronic disease management, and supporting the critical role of primary care physicians is unparalleled. Powered by technological advancements, advanced data analytics, and early evidence-based medicine, the aspirational healthcare model is proving the once-thought impossible is within reach.

Located in a unique and challenging healthcare delivery location, Alaska, the Nuka System of Care has experienced its own challenges. The foundation for aspirational healthcare was built through perseverance, adaptation, and applying a large dose of personal touch. This model, which manages costs through self-accountability without compromising quality and is driven by a transparent, collaborative approach, is getting the attention of the right stakeholders—CEOs.

This book provides powerful insights for CEOs to embrace in their healthcare transformation journey.

E. Heidi Cottle
Senior Vice President of Cost Containment Strategies for NFP,
an Aon Company

INTRODUCTION

My goal is to shine a bright light on the best healthcare system in the world. I want to create a world where people think of healthcare as a partner to help them do what they want to do.

Dear business leaders,

One of the most important aspects of your business is one that you're likely not paying enough attention to—healthcare.

But the truth is healthcare is more than just a business expense. It's one of your highest costs of doing business, and as things currently are, you're not getting your money's worth and neither are your employees. If you're not actively working toward creating better healthcare for your employees at a lower cost, you're being taken advantage of by the healthcare system.

Did you know that healthcare is one of the largest industries in America?[1] In fact, it accounted for approximately 17% of our country's GDP at $4.5 trillion, in 2022.[2] It's hard to wrap your head around numbers that large, so for reference, that makes the American healthcare system the fourth largest economy in the world, only behind the entire economies of the U.S., China, and Japan. The amount Americans spend on healthcare alone is pretty staggering, but it's even more shocking when you account for the amount of that money that goes to waste—spending that has nothing to do with providing healthcare services. Out of the over $4 trillion spent on healthcare, $2 trillion was waste,[3] a number approximately the size of the entire GDP of Russia.

When we start talking about numbers above the millions, most people don't realize just how large those numbers really are. For reference, if we compared these numbers to time rather than money, one million seconds ago was 11 days ago; one billion seconds ago was more than 31 years ago; and *one trillion* seconds ago was more than *31,000 years* ago.

Even if these shocking numbers are new to you, I'm sure you were already aware that the American healthcare system is riddled with problems—high costs with astronomical amounts of waste, poor health outcomes, and a misalignment of priorities. These three traits have become characteristic of the industry. And it's even likely you know someone in your personal life who has suffered as a result of these deep-rooted problems. The reality is that healthcare is extremely personal and has a tangible impact on all of our lives.

I began looking for other healthcare options after my career in hospital administration left me looking for better solutions. I'd been a hospital administrator for many years and made a lot of money doing it.

There came a point in my hospital administrator career where my viewpoint allowed me to recognize so many of the problems in the healthcare industry that I felt I had to do something about it.

My success as a hospital administrator was measured not in the health outcomes of the hospital patients, but by the number of beds I was able to keep full to bring in more money for the hospital. Essentially, my job was to scheme every day to work against my customer—the people paying for healthcare services. It was the ethical problem this posed that eventually drove me to leave that career path and seek an alternative to provide better, less expensive healthcare.

Even while healthcare costs have risen, the quality of the services provided hasn't improved. In fact, despite medical advancements, the quality of care patients receive has declined as average appointment times have dwindled to only a few minutes for each patient.

The high cost of healthcare combined with the poor quality of service leads many patients to avoid seeking treatment until a problem becomes unmanageable, when the opportunity to prevent or fix the problem may have already passed. In healthcare, treating a sick population is much more expensive than maintaining the health of a healthy population, but the system isn't set up to do that—in fact, it's set up to do the opposite: making more money from illness.

We have a sick-care system, not a healthcare system.

In the documentary *Escape Fire*,[4] one doctor made a statement that demonstrates many of the problems in U.S. healthcare: "If I spend five minutes with you and then put in one of these stents, I probably get paid $1,500; for me to spend 45 minutes with a patient to try to figure out what their true problem is, I probably get paid $15. It's a completely irrational system."

The system is built to drive a money-making machine, not to improve the health of the population.

One of the leading causes of death in the U.S. is medical errors.[5] Primary care providers don't have the time to focus on what the patient really needs. Their job is to serve the administrators of the hospitals. The system is designed to fill hospital beds. And that's not the fault of doctors—it's about a misalignment of priorities and incentives.

While the problems with the U.S. healthcare system are numerous, I want to point out three that contribute to the high costs employers and their employees pay.

1. **Misaligned health outcome incentives**: Hospitals' incentives are to fill up beds and to fit as many appointments as possible into their schedules, leading to lower quality of care and treating illnesses rather than preventing them.

2. **Insurance companies make more money as healthcare costs go up**: Because in most cases 85% of premiums must go toward paying claims, insurance companies grow their profits by encouraging the costs of healthcare services to rise.

3. **Brokers' incentives are not aligned with employers' interests**: Insurance brokers often make more money as insurance costs go up.

These three problems are at the root of many of the other problems within the healthcare industry. They result in high costs, poor quality of care, and a system that's confusing to navigate. Physicians are unhappy with their jobs, overworked and underpaid, and unable to provide the level of care they want for their patients. Patients are often disengaged from their healthcare and avoid seeking care until they become ill and treatment becomes a necessity.

Are those the outcomes you want for your employees? Of course not. You want to provide them with a benefit that gives them the care they need and contributes to a happy and healthy workforce.

A BETTER OPTION FOR HEALTHCARE

As the cost of healthcare continuously rises, the financial burden falls on both patients (your employees) and you, their employer, who pays for their healthcare plans.

> For many companies, healthcare is their second-highest cost of doing business.

As the second-highest cost of doing business, you have an interest in keeping the cost of healthcare down, but for most CEOs, healthcare is a "get it and forget it" item on their checklist, which they typically hand off to their HR department. Too often I hear CEOs say that it's just a cost of doing business and they will pay whatever they have to in order to offer good benefits to their employees.

Now more than ever, it's time to take back the reins of healthcare decisions to offer your employees better benefits and spend a lot less money doing so. Yes, you can offer better benefits for less! Insist on creating an employee health plan dashboard that shows you how well your investment is working in easy-to-read graphs showing the metrics you're tracking. If you are the leader of your company, it's not okay to have a "get it and forget it" mentality. Expect more from your benefits team, expect more from your benefits consultant, and expect more from the healthcare system. That starts by setting expectations and using a dashboard to monitor your investment. This has to be driven by the CEO. It's time to make healthcare work for you!

In my current role, I get the chance to speak in front of CEOs on a regular basis. And I love to ask them the question, "Why do you buy healthcare for your employees? As the customer, what do you want?" They almost always say the following four things, in this order:

1. I want to attract and retain top talent.
2. I want a healthy, productive workforce, which makes my product better. My clients are happier when my employees are healthy and productive.
3. I want my employees to be satisfied with the healthcare I offer them.
4. I want it to be more affordable.

The reason you pay for health insurance isn't just because the government requires you to. The penalty for failing to provide medical insurance is far less than the cost of providing it. The truth is you want your employees to be healthy and happy, and you need to offer a competitive benefits package to attract and retain your best talent. On a deeper level, you probably care about your employees. But the traditional U.S. healthcare system exploits both employers who purchase insurance and employees who use the healthcare services. As a result, whether you're the employer or the patient, healthcare costs tend to feel like something outside of your control, even when the quality of the service you receive for your money is extremely low.

It doesn't have to be this way.

Healthcare doesn't have to cost so much. It can meet the financial and medical needs of your employees and better serve everyone involved.

You might say, "Darrell, that is a pie-in-the-sky idea. There is no way that can happen." I'm here to tell you—in fact, I wrote this book to tell you—that it's possible. And it's not an experimental approach. It's a system that's been around for over 20 years.

You can offer better healthcare for your employees *and* save your company money. There is a new way of doing healthcare that provides personalized service and eliminates the unnecessary waste so prevalent in the industry.

I've always liked W. Edwards Deming's method for continuous quality improvement (CQI)—a system based around four simple steps:

- Identify who is your customer.

- Identify what delights your customer.

- Measure the processes that most impact delighting your customer.

- When you find variance in a process, get the people closest to the process to improve it and eliminate the variance.

As the CEO of your company, you probably already apply these simple CQI business strategies to every aspect of your business—except healthcare.

It's time to approach healthcare the same way you approach every other problem in your business. Healthcare is a problem to solve, not just a purchase to be made. The solution starts with you, the CEO, waking up and realizing you do have the power to do something about it.

CEOs, you are the customer of the healthcare industry. You may not feel like you are, but you are. As the customer, it's time to step up and make healthcare work for you. Start by setting expectations and then expect the feedback—the monitors and the dashboard—to show you how well it's working.

After asking over a thousand CEOs across the country what they wanted and listening to them list the four desires mentioned, I have yet to find a single CEO who is measuring to see if they are getting what they want. That is your problem as a CEO to fix—no one else's.

Almost 30 years ago, I left the treatment side of healthcare to see if I could help balance the scales for employers, the customers of healthcare. I wanted to find a way to apply CQI to the process of purchasing healthcare. What I have found is you feel powerless against the prevalent healthcare industry in America. However, the fact of the matter is that you hold all the power.

I knew that I needed to show CEOs proof that there is another way and that you can expect more from the healthcare you purchase.

HOW NUKA TRANSFORMED HEALTHCARE

I began looking for other solutions, and eventually I discovered the Nuka System of Care. Nuka is an Alaska Native word used to mean strong, giant structures and living things.

The Nuka System of Care is a healthcare system created by Southcentral Foundation, an organization that serves about 70,000 Alaska Native and American Indian people living in the municipality of Anchorage, Matanuska-Susitna Borough, and nearby villages.

This was the beginning of the model we call *aspirational healthcare*, and 25 years later, Nuka is now recognized internationally as one of the world's premier healthcare systems, with some of the highest levels of patient satisfaction. And here's the most remarkable thing—they cut their healthcare costs in half and accomplished what no one thought was possible: they have created a healthcare system that actually works for its customers and improves health outcomes dramatically.

What the Nuka System of Care (the Model for Aspirational Healthcare) Has Accomplished

- 97% customer satisfaction

- 63% decrease in hospitalizations (2000-2004)

- Significant cost savings represented by decreased use of higher-cost services, such as hospital stays, specialty services, and emergency department visits, as well as more efficient use of primary care resources

---

How did they do it? First of all, they built a relationship-based healthcare system around the customer. I'm going to say that again: *relationship-based healthcare*.

While science is an important part of healthcare, the healthcare system needs to be based on human relationships. The Nuka System of Care figured that out and made that the priority.

They built an incredibly effective primary care system based on relationships. They developed a team of doctors, nurses, and case managers whose first priority was to get to know the story of every patient they worked with. These relationships are about more than just fixing people when they break. Instead, they partner with and support them on their journeys to wellness.

Every level of care is coordinated to meet the needs of the patient, because the system is built around the customer. In fact, they never use the word "patient." They refer to the people they serve as "customer-owners."

> **It is called an aspirational healthcare model because it's not a reactive system meant to care for the sick—it's about journeying with people to help them live life to its fullest so they can reach their aspirations.**

Does this sound revolutionary? Absolutely. It's not how most healthcare systems work today, but you can accomplish for your own employees what the Nuka System has accomplished. As an employer, it's all about how you spend your money and what kind of healthcare you choose to offer your employees. And when you offer aspirational healthcare (AH), it will be far better than traditional healthcare plans at attracting and retaining top talent, as well as proactively addressing your employees' physical and mental health needs, which increases employee satisfaction overall. And the best part of all? It costs about half as much.

Since I first discovered the Nuka System, I have attended their conference multiple times to learn from the people who built the system and discover ways to bring the aspirational healthcare model to more people. We created our company Aspirational Healthcare, a BLLC social impact company, with the goal of improving human health. Southcentral Foundation has been very supportive of our efforts to promote their healthcare model—they want to encourage others to use it in hopes that the healthcare system in America, and systems all over the world, can be transformed by it.

Aspirational Healthcare, BLLC, is a subsidiary of my company Orriant (pronounced to rhyme with *client*). It helps employers offer better healthcare to their employees while significantly lowering their costs. We use the term "aspirational healthcare" to describe the systems we help employers build, which are modeled off the very successful methods Southcentral Foundation used.

What makes aspirational healthcare different from traditional healthcare? Among other things, it uses subscription-based primary care focused on relationships and coaching to help customers reach their personal goals and aspirations. By having a trusting relationship with their primary care provider, individuals experience a whole new level of healthcare focused on the whole person. And amazingly, AH results in significant cost savings for both the customer and their employer.

The beauty of AH is that by establishing strong relationships between provider and patient, many health issues can be prevented or managed before they become serious, creating better overall health outcomes. The power of this relationship-based model combined with regular coaching has been shown to be incredibly effective and results in high levels of patient satisfaction—it's akin to having a trusted family member as your primary care provider. If your dad was a doctor, you wouldn't hesitate to call him as soon as you had a health question. And when a specialist is needed, your care is coordinated at all levels to ensure you are being taken care of and that all the providers are talking to each other.

One of the most important things to understand is that while aspirational healthcare can save you and your employees a significant amount of money, some employees will want to keep their current providers, and that's okay—you can still give them that option. Part of why aspirational healthcare works so well is it empowers patients to care for their own health by giving them choices, and it's important to allow them to choose whether they want it. However, you can incentivize them to use the AH model and demonstrate how it can benefit them. Those who do make the switch will benefit from improved health and financial incentives while saving significant costs, and your business will save significantly as well.

I'm certain you have plenty of questions about how this model can work, and I assure you that we'll address them in the coming chapters. I founded Orriant to help people access a better model of healthcare and make it work for their companies and their people, but it's possible to do it yourself using the steps I'll outline in this book. My goal is to educate people on what healthcare can look like and inspire them to take steps toward a better healthcare system for the U.S., starting with employers. And believe it or not, you have the power to do that.

As a CEO, you have a pivotal role in enhancing healthcare for your employees and their families, as well as your own.

The key to transforming healthcare in the U.S. starts with those who control the financial resources—the purchasers.

It's time to demand more value for your healthcare expenditure. Instead of settling for traditional models that create deficits, consider investing in an aspirational healthcare approach that emphasizes proactive well-being and substantial savings.

CEOs, as major stakeholders in healthcare, wield significant influence over the direction of the U.S. healthcare system. Through aspirational healthcare, we can forge a path toward a healthier nation, starting within our own organizations. It's an opportunity for business leaders to be at the forefront of a healthier future for all.

It's high time to expect more and make healthcare work for you and your employees.

—Darrell T. Moon

CHAPTER 1

Holding Healthcare Accountable

My role as a hospital administrator gave me a very clear view of the way the U.S. healthcare system works. I was very lucky to be running two healthcare facilities by the age of 26 as the CFO/controller of both of those facilities, and I worked my way up to becoming a hospital administrator very quickly.

I broke into the industry in a rather nontraditional way. Although I was preparing for a master's degree in health administration (MHA), I visited an administrator in the nearby town of Orem, Utah, and asked to volunteer in the offices to get some experience. He gave me the amazing opportunity to help their hospital figure out their new technology—they'd just bought an IBM personal computer.

I built a strong relationship with that administrator and when the opportunity came up for him to work at a new hospital that was being built in town, he asked me to be the CFO/controller of that new hospital. It was the opportunity of a lifetime. I took the role, still working on my undergraduate degree in finance, and continued working that job as I went on to earn my master of health administration at Brigham Young University, taking classes in the evenings.

Eventually, I got to run 10 different hospitals across the country, most of them owned by one of the largest hospital companies in the U.S., Hospital Corporation of America.

During those years, I became very disillusioned with my own industry. I realized that the primary objective of my job was to fill my hospital, which did not serve the interests of my customers—those who pay for the majority of healthcare: employers. Those customers wanted their employees to be healthy and productive, not in hospital beds. I spent a lot of time pondering that perplexity.

The truth is the American healthcare system is, in many ways, a financial machine. When I was born in 1960, the healthcare industry represented 5% of our country's gross domestic product (GDP). Within 60 short years, it has grown to 17% of our GDP. That is almost 400% growth. Every other industry has had to make room for this exploding industry that is not being held accountable.

Through my roles as CEO, COO, and CFO of various hospitals, I estimated that close to half of the total cost of running a hospital is spent on services associated with billing and collecting money from insurance companies, which include being accredited. Something is very wrong with an industry that has to spend so much money just collecting their money.

Many people believe that the insurance industry is holding healthcare providers accountable. But the insurance industry actually benefits from that reputation and hides behind it. In fact, the insurance companies are often the cause of many of the problems in the industry. Think about all the terrible stories of how insurance companies won't approve life-saving treatments and medications. Who is holding the insurance companies accountable? No one.

You may assume that it's in the insurance companies' best interests to keep the cost of health services low, because the less they have to pay providers, the more money they'll make. Well, here's one of the biggest secrets of the healthcare industry: it is actually just the opposite.

The Affordable Care Act (ACA) of 2010 created a requirement that, in most cases, 85% of what insurance companies collect in premiums has to go toward paying healthcare claims. If less goes toward claims, the insurance company has to return the money to the customers. Hence, the only way for an insurance company's profits to increase is for healthcare costs to go up.

If you own stock shares in UnitedHealthcare, a health insurance company owned by UnitedHealth Group Incorporated—the world's eleventh-largest company by revenue and the largest healthcare company by revenue—the value of those shares only increases if healthcare costs go up. Insurance companies, like most companies, exist to increase the value of their owners' shares. And the only way for them to do that is to increase the cost of healthcare, so the 15% that doesn't go toward paying claims continues to grow larger.

Why have healthcare costs exploded far above any other part of the American economy? The customers are the only ones who can hold the industry accountable, and they're not doing that.

To be clear, it is not the healthcare providers making it explode. Most healthcare providers in the U.S. are amazing and dedicated individuals who want what's best for their patients. It is the middlemen and unnecessary waste in the system that have exploded the cost of healthcare.

Some estimates show that only 27% of this gigantic industry goes toward paying the actual providers. The rest goes toward waste, fraud, abuse, and overhead.

An article in the *Journal of American Medical Association* (JAMA)[6] reported that the United States spends twice as much on healthcare as any other country. Yet the health outcomes are not even close to the top. When you observe this discrepancy, it is not difficult to believe how healthcare in the U.S. could be half as expensive. It is the lack of accountability on the part of private payers, like employers, that has created this discrepancy.

FOUR SECRETS TO SAVING TREMENDOUSLY ON HEALTHCARE

The healthcare system is massive and complicated, and there's no single factor you can point to as a source of the vast waste. However, when it comes to your costs as an employer, there are four major ways the healthcare system extracts money from employers. When you understand them, it's not difficult to make adjustments to create significant savings, often between 40-60% of your total healthcare spending.

The aspirational healthcare model directly addresses these four issues. In doing so, AH is able to significantly reduce costs while also providing a higher level of care.

1. **Feeding the dragon**: Most patients enter the healthcare system through their primary care providers, which are usually owned and operated by hospitals and healthcare systems that are motivated not to provide excellent health outcomes

but to fill up hospital beds and create as much profit as possible. By giving people access to a whole new form of primary care that isn't owned by hospitals, you stop feeding the dragon and provide a better healthcare experience from the beginning (see chapter 7).

2. **Price elasticity**: Most people are not aware of the incredible amount of price elasticity within the healthcare industry. When a patient is sent to secondary care, such as imaging or a specialist, they're usually sent wherever the system wants them to go, such as other healthcare system-owned specialists, imaging centers, ambulatory surgical centers, or hospitals. Often, those providers are not the most cost-effective and may not provide the best outcomes. The companies that own the funnels control where patients go for healthcare. The elasticity of prices within healthcare is massive. You can go to two neighboring hospitals and find that one with a three-star rating charges $70,000 for a procedure while another one with a five-star rating charges $7,000 for the same procedure. By simply navigating people toward the best outcome providers, you can save enormous amounts of money (see chapter 8).

3. **Egregious drug profits**: A great deal of money is wasted between the manufacturers of drugs and the pharmacies that dispense them, and this is a result of pharmacy benefit management companies (PBMs). These companies siphon money out of our pockets and significantly raise the costs of drugs. By changing the way you create health plans for your

employees, you can bypass those egregious profits and access prescriptions at a much lower cost (see chapter 9).

4. **Lifestyle**: The vast majority of all healthcare costs (87.5%) can be traced back to lifestyle. The traditional healthcare system does very little to help people develop healthy lifestyles. Aspirational healthcare is about giving people support to reach their dreams, changing behavior not by telling them what to do but by guiding and supporting them toward their own goals. This approach to healthcare creates more effective lifestyle changes and has a long-term impact on healthcare costs by reducing the need for more extensive care overall (see chapter 4).

We will cover each of these items in greater detail in the coming chapters, but for now, knowing how the systems at play within healthcare are built to take your money will help you understand that effective change to hold healthcare accountable *is within your power*.

HOW DID WE GET HERE?

To understand many of the problems with the American healthcare system, you need to understand how it came to be.

At the end of WWII, the War Labor Board put freezes on employee salaries across the country because a lack of labor supply was driving prices up. A year later, the IRS began to allow employers to deduct health insurance if they purchased it for their employees. So, companies began purchasing health insurance for their employees and getting group insurance benefits—previously, insurance was purchased mainly through individual policies.

It only took about a decade before the majority of Americans were on a group plan. Health insurance was an attractive hiring incentive employers could offer. As a result, insurance agents and brokers began selling group health insurance. Brokers play an important role of representing the buyers in the healthcare system, but because employers don't hold them accountable, the misalignments within the broker community have become a big part of the problem.

Auto insurance, which is still purchased by individuals, hasn't exploded in price the way health insurance has because auto insurance companies still have to compete for the business of individual customers. But with health insurance, the buyers (employers) select a broker who goes and gets bids from the various insurance companies and brings back the bad news every year that costs are going up and benefits are going down. The employer then chooses the best of all the bad options. They aren't measuring to see if the money they are spending is accomplishing their business objectives, and no one is being held accountable to make sure that happens.

The state of American healthcare can't just be blamed on the idea that we're a "sick nation." It's true that healthcare would cost less if people lived healthier lifestyles, but the system doesn't support its people to be healthier. In fact, it makes more money on sick people than on healthy people. There's no financial incentive to keep people healthy.

HOW CAN WE HOLD THE HEALTHCARE SYSTEM ACCOUNTABLE?

We all want a better healthcare system—one that provides us with the kind of care that helps us accomplish our goals, maintains and improves our health, is reliably there for us when we have a catastrophic need, and is affordable.

While that vision may not seem realistic based on the current healthcare system, the truth is it doesn't have to be this way.

CEOs have the power to hold the healthcare industry accountable.

Every CEO knows the simple principle that what gets measured gets managed. The same thing applies in healthcare, and yet many businesses are not measuring the healthcare they provide beyond how much it costs them.

As a speaker for Vistage, the world's top executive coaching organization, I have had the privilege of speaking to over 100 groups of CEOs around the country in order to help them discover ways to improve their healthcare offerings while cutting their costs. But despite the fact that healthcare accounts for the second-largest cost of doing business, none of those CEOs were measuring or monitoring whether that cost was working to accomplish their business objectives. No one was expecting a dashboard that monitors the effectiveness of their investment in healthcare.

When I share this insight with CEOs, they often have a moment of realization, as if a new understanding has suddenly clicked for them. *Where's my dashboard?*

Wouldn't it be easy to send out a survey to your employees every year with a few simple questions to ascertain how well the company's investment in health benefits is working to retain them? The answers would easily reveal whether that investment is helping you accomplish your business objectives or if it needs to be adjusted.

"What gets measured gets managed."
–Peter Drucker

The healthcare system must be held accountable to work for the customer. This is perhaps the most fundamental problem with the traditional healthcare industry. Too often, its accountability is to profit, not to customers or patients.

So where do you start in creating accountability? It begins with aligning your team with your interests. Expect your healthcare team to create dashboards for you to monitor your goals. Hold people accountable.

The majority of CEOs hand off the decisions on purchasing health insurance to their human resources (HR) department, who then work with a broker to find a group plan. Very few CEOs recognize, incentivize, or reward their HR departments for helping them reach their business objectives, and even fewer of them align their benefits broker/advisor with their business objectives. Those who manage the health benefits for companies should receive incentives based on how well the company meets its goals.

I like to ask CEOs if they have a benefits broker to represent their company and reach out to insurance companies to get competitive bids every year. Most of them do. But when I ask them how that broker gets paid, their general response is that the broker gets a commission from the insurance company.

Then I ask them this: "So when your costs go up, your benefits broker often gets a raise? Their compensation is never tied to whether you're achieving your business goals?" The answer is almost always "correct."

It doesn't have to work that way. Did you know that as a CEO, you can sign a fee-based contract with a benefits broker or consultant so they get paid directly from you? You can stipulate that they receive no commissions from the premiums. If the insurance companies won't strip the commissions out of the cost, require that they be transparent about those commissions and recognize it as part of their compensation. The key is to build incentives and bonuses into that contract based on how well the company meets its business objectives.

This has now become the gold standard for working with a benefits advisor. Insist on it immediately. If your benefits advisor refuses, *fire them on the spot.* By saying no, they basically just told you that they don't work for you, they work for the broken system, and they want you to stay in it.

CEOs do this kind of alignment with every other part of their businesses, but they almost never do this to manage their healthcare expenses. Those expenses often represent 10-20% of the total costs of running their businesses.

Even if your broker is already getting commissions based on the number of employees you have rather than the price of the premium, it's still in your best interest to have them aligned with your business objectives and working for you. I know of brokers and benefit consultants who are achieving unbelievable results for their clients using this method. The average health insurance cost per employee for U.S. businesses in 2023 was $13,800 per year, and companies with fee-based broker contracts are often spending half of that amount.

When CEOs align the healthcare system to work for them and start by aligning their internal and external teams to work toward the company's business objectives, new doors open to options that have never been explored before. The benefits are much better than they have ever been. The costs go down and the benefits go up.

CEOs need to take an active role in driving this alignment. And it doesn't take a lot of time. Simply have your team create a dashboard that tracks your progress on the goals that matter to you—your objectives for purchasing healthcare.

WHAT GETS MEASURED GETS MANAGED

In order to measure how well your company is meeting your business objectives regarding healthcare, you must first define those objectives.

Why do you purchase healthcare for your employees? Although most CEOs tell me that attracting and retaining top talent and creating a healthy productive workforce is at the top of their list, that doesn't mean it is the same for every company.

One of my client companies delineated their goal to retain top talent for just their key positions. They identified positions within their company where turnover would be devastating to the company, while there were other positions where regular turnover was not a problem. In designing their efforts to measure employee satisfaction, they were very intentional about getting feedback that was broken down into those two categories. I'm not saying I necessarily agree with their strategy, but the point is that not every company has the same goals and objectives.

Once your objectives have been defined, you must measure outcomes to determine whether you're meeting those objectives.

If your objective is to attract and retain top talent, that's very easy to measure: You can use a survey with a few simple questions asking employees to rate how well they agree with the following statements:

- I am satisfied with the healthcare system available through my benefits.

- My healthcare benefits are a positive influence on my continuing to work here.

- The healthcare system is easy to use and navigate.

- The healthcare system is there when I need it.

- The healthcare system provides quality/effective services.

Ask your team to create a dashboard that tells you how your company is doing in each of these areas.

For a business objective of a healthy and productive workforce, measuring success can be more difficult, especially since results may be subjective. Often, employers measure well-being, broken down into eight categories, using short surveys:

- Social

- Emotional

- Occupational

- Intellectual

- Financial

- Physical

- Environmental

- Nutritional

Options for measurement also include health risk appraisals, though these only give a snapshot of the workforce's health at a single point in time. Short, regular pulse surveys offer a better view of health trends, which allows you to make adjustments as needed.

Another common strategy to measure employee health is offering annual biometric screenings. This is a more objective measurement, and it is only focused on physical health. Biometric screenings often include blood pressure, body fat percentage, body mass index, cholesterol ratio, and glucose levels. Measuring these biometrics from year to year can show important trends in overall physical health within the workforce.

It's also possible to measure employee productivity, and systems for this vary. However, it's rare for employers to reward their benefits managers, brokers, or HR departments based on improvements in productivity. If one of the primary business objectives for purchasing healthcare benefits is to enhance employee productivity, these should be tied together.

Measuring healthcare costs is simple but should be done every year. Your costs should not be increasing every year—in fact, you should start expecting annual decreases if you align your healthcare to work for you.

What are you measuring? What data are you analyzing relative to your health benefit plan? Are you looking at utilization and gaps in care reports? The most important data to measure is whether you are accomplishing the business objectives for why you buy healthcare, not where the gaps in care are. When you do, you'll be far more effective at reaching your objectives.

Clarify the business objectives for why you're purchasing healthcare. Then measure them, monitor them, and make the healthcare system work for you, because right now you're working for it. It does not take a lot of effort to expect a dashboard.

CHAPTER 2

The Aspirational Solution Is Here

The Nuka System of Care pioneered the aspirational healthcare model, and they are now recognized as one of the world's leading examples of healthcare redesign. I've already told you a bit about Nuka, but how did they develop their system? What problems were they trying to solve?

After decades as "beneficiaries" of an inefficient, underfunded federal healthcare system, Alaska Native and American Indian people were ready for radical changes in their healthcare experience. Southcentral Foundation's origin story began with groups of determined Alaska Native and American Indian people coming together and advocating for a voice in program planning and operations.

As a result of their persistence, Congress passed the Indian Self-Determination and Education Assistance Act in 1975. It acknowledged that federal domination of these health and education programs was causing more harm than good. The legislation gave Tribes greater control over the funding, which affected their community health and well-being. Encouraged by this change, Alaska Native people established Southcentral Foundation (SCF) on

March 8, 1982, under the Tribal authority of Cook Inlet Region, Inc. The vision was a healthcare system rooted in cultural strengths that could improve health and change lives. A series of amendments and other legislation throughout the '80s and '90s allowed Tribes to take self-determination several steps further to own and operate their programs. At last, by the late '90s, Alaska Native people in southcentral Alaska had full control as the "customer-owners" of the healthcare system.

They did something no other healthcare system had ever done: they asked their customers what they wanted.

After many months of surveying the Alaska Native Community, Southcentral Foundation learned what their customers wanted from a healthcare system. Their first goal was to realign how healthcare worked by bringing the patient into focus as the decision-maker for their own healthcare. They called patients "customers" or "customer-owners" to make it clear that providers and administrators were providing services based on what customers wanted.

The customers said they did *not* want a paternalistic healthcare system that told them what to do. Instead, they wanted a healthcare system that partnered with them on their journeys through life and supported them in reaching their aspirations. They called their system *aspirational healthcare* to focus their efforts on helping their customers reach their personal aspirations.

Instead of investing dollars into intensive care units and hospitals, they invested in a whole new form of primary care, which would serve as a new *front door* to healthcare. They created a primary care team made up of a primary care provider, a nurse case manager, a medical assistant, behavioral health consultant, and a support person. They assigned each of these teams to small groups of customer-owners. Their primary responsibility was to develop a trusting relationship with everyone they served—to be a friend, a trusted confidant, and a coach—and support each person in their efforts to reach their destinations. These relationships were founded on cultural sensitivity and respect.

It turns out that relationships are far more important than creating a perfect treatment plan. What good is a well-designed treatment plan if the individual does not implement it? The vast majority of what impacts the health of an individual is up to the individual.

SCF surrounded this core primary care team with an ancillary team of professionals including a pharmacist, a dietician, a certified nurse midwife, and a community resource specialist. Together, the focused primary team and the ancillary team formed a comprehensive team of healthcare professionals to support customer-owners. They created a behavioral-focused, relationship-based healthcare system wrapped around the customer.

Customer-owners can message their primary care team via the patient portal 24/7, with team members responding during clinic hours. For urgent care or emergency services outside of primary care hours, customer-owners can visit SCF staff face-to-face seven days a week through Fast Track in the Emergency Services department. This customer-centric primary care team is expected to ensure same-day access to care and to coordinate care at all levels of complexity, whether in primary care or in the hospital.

SCF's Nuka System of Care is built around the understanding that personal, long-term, accountable relationships with customer-owners, their families, and their communities are the key to making a difference in the ongoing choices and habits that drive health and well-being.

To reinforce their goal of long-term, ongoing care, they incorporated regular evaluations of the quality of the health outcomes they were achieving. They used HEDIS, a widely used performance evaluation tool in the healthcare industry, which stands for Healthcare Effectiveness Data and Information Set.

Today, the SCF Nuka System of Care is nationally and internationally recognized as one of the most innovative healthcare systems in the world.

The following are the outcomes of this whole new model of healthcare:

- Nuka is the only healthcare system to be a two-time winner of the U.S. President's prestigious Malcolm Baldrige Award for Quality (2011 and 2017).

- 97% of customer-owners are satisfied (FY 2023).

- 91% of employees are satisfied (FY 2023).

- SCF has seen significant improvements in population health, measured against NCQA HEDIS benchmarks. Most of SCF's clinical performance measures are currently greater than the HEDIS 75th percentile and some are above the 90th percentile.

- They have achieved lower costs through reduced hospital stays and emergency department visits, reduced use of specialty services, and more efficient use of primary care resources.

- They've decreased ER visits by 44% (2000-2004).

- The appointment schedule went from four weeks out to same-day availability.

- The behavioral waitlist went from 1,300 to zero.

- The call wait time went from two minutes to 30 seconds.

- They've reduced hospital discharges by 38% (2000–2021).

- They've reduced specialty clinic visits by 58% and sustained that reduction for 10 years.

Representatives from 45 countries and 2,950 organizations have visited Anchorage, Alaska, to learn about the Nuka System of Care. Organizations like the National Healthcare Group Singapore and First Nations Health Authority Canada have designed many of their systems around this inspiring model.

Southcentral Foundation has proven that transforming healthcare to focus on relationship-based primary care creates a healthcare system that is light-years better than the current system offered across most of America.

HOW ASPIRATIONAL HEALTHCARE CREATES RESULTS

Aspirational healthcare, meaning any system following the tenets of the Nuka System of Care, has the potential to cut your healthcare costs significantly. At the same time, it can help you meet your other business objectives, whether that's improving employee health and productivity, attracting and retaining talent, or something else. How does it do that?

The results are achieved through three fundamental principles:

1. **Alignment**

   Alignment means getting the healthcare system to work for the customer. The customer is twofold—employers, who make health insurance purchasing decisions, and employees, the patients themselves. This starts with measuring and managing the aspects that make a difference in costs and health outcomes to eliminate wasteful spending and ensure that the best quality of care is provided by aligning incentives with the customers' (and providers') interests.

2. **Choice**

   Giving people choices in their healthcare creates better long-term health outcomes and makes them more likely to follow through on achieving their goals. The concept of "compliance" is replaced with offering choices and helping customers find internal motivation for healthcare changes they want to make to achieve their goals. The healthcare system should be compliant with the wishes of the individual, the family, and the community, not the other way around. Instead of trying to get people to do what healthcare professionals want them to do, healthcare can be focused on helping individuals accomplish their goals in life.

3. **Relationship**

   Relationships where patients know their providers and have continual and personalized support on their health journeys help people reach their goals and create better long-term health outcomes. The trust and accountability established through personal relationships and coaching has been shown to be incredibly effective.

These three principles are vital to the success of the AH model, and they address the root causes of many of the problems that exist within the traditional healthcare industry. It's a fundamentally different approach to healthcare, which is what makes it so successful, but it doesn't work without these three aspects. Expect to have a dashboard that helps you monitor how well your company is addressing each of these three areas.

We'll go into more detail about the principles of choice and relationship in later chapters, but I want to start by discussing alignment. Creating alignment is the first step toward aspirational healthcare.

The lack of alignment starts with the business leader who fails to define their objectives. Without objectives, leaders fail to measure whether they're accomplishing what they want through purchasing healthcare. Money flows out, but no accountability comes back. Business leaders have the unique position of power to influence healthcare by creating accountability.

Define your objectives, put in place ways to measure your progress, and hold people accountable to help you achieve your objectives.

UNDERSTANDING THE ASPIRATIONAL HEALTHCARE MODEL

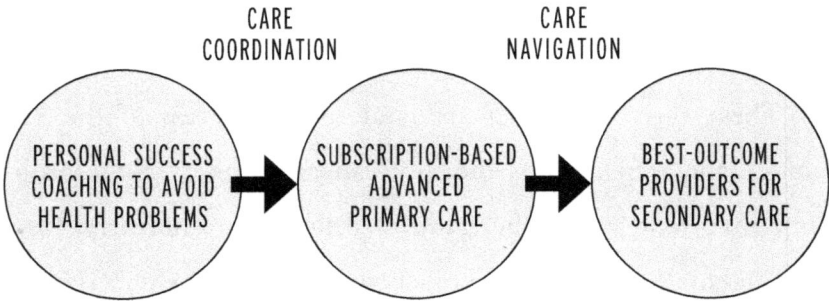

CARE COORDINATION   CARE NAVIGATION

PERSONAL SUCCESS COACHING TO AVOID HEALTH PROBLEMS → SUBSCRIPTION-BASED ADVANCED PRIMARY CARE → BEST-OUTCOME PROVIDERS FOR SECONDARY CARE

I realize that aspirational healthcare may seem difficult to wrap your head around if all you've ever known is traditional healthcare dominated by conventional health insurance. Let me break it down for you.

Aspirational healthcare isn't a one-size-fits-all solution—instead, it's customizable based on the needs of your company and your employees.

Aspirational healthcare is an overall design of a health plan that fosters a focus on the customer and their needs. By focusing on the needs of the customer, the plan design creates tremendous savings.

Let me describe the aspirational healthcare model in three basic elements.

1. **Personal Success Coaching**

   First of all, just as much emphasis is put on keeping people well as on fixing them when they get sick. Right now, we build healthcare to catch people when they fall off a cliff and make money fixing them so they can get back on their journey. What if healthcare was just as much focused on keeping us from falling off the cliff in the first place?

   For many people, good health can be described as the absence of health problems that stand in the way of what they want to do. One of the most successful ways to help people accomplish their goals and stay healthy is to offer the support of a personal success coach.

Imagine a healthcare system where everyone has a coach in their corner to help them reach their destinations, goals, dreams, and aspirations in life. The coach is not there to tell them what to do, but rather to build trust and uncover genuine life aspirations, then support that individual in reaching their goals.

What made Nuka so successful was centering healthcare around relationships. This approach creates motivation from the individual's own aspirations to help them make healthier lifestyle choices that prevent illnesses and lead to better overall health outcomes. For more information about coaching and relationship-based healthcare, see chapter 4.

2. **Subscription-Based Advanced Primary Care (APC)**

   Next, the AH model recommends the use of *advanced primary care*, discussed in more detail in chapter 7. In this model, independent advanced primary care providers develop relationships with their patients and are paid to keep them well. Rather than getting paid for treating problems, these providers are paid a fixed amount every month for every member in their practice. Their goals and incentives are aligned to keep their members healthy and give them immediate access to the best care possible.

   These providers are independent and not owned by the healthcare system. This results in tremendous savings by not feeding the traditional networks of providers. APC providers don't act as funnels sending patients into healthcare systems that aren't accountable to cost and quality. Instead, they focus on doing what's best for the patient.

Offering APC allows members of your health plan the opportunity to engage in primary care that builds relationships, keeps them healthy, supports them in reaching their life goals, and offers immediate access to care.

3. **Best Outcome Providers for Secondary Care**
   The third element of the AH model is helping members find providers who achieve the highest level of health outcomes when secondary care is needed. This can be done through a care navigator to direct members to providers based on cost and quality data.

   Secondary care providers, such as specialists, imaging centers, surgical centers, and hospitals *should* have to compete on cost and quality. However, the traditional system avoids steering patients toward particular providers, which allows hospital-owned physicians to direct patients within their own hospital's system, regardless of outcomes.

   The more customer-focused approach is to look for providers who achieve better outcomes. Better outcomes naturally result in tremendous savings because the best providers are almost always less expensive as a result of fewer complications that would require more care.

   Healthcare transparency laws make cost and quality information available to the public. By providing care navigation based on this information, this model forces healthcare systems to compete based on providing quality services at a good price, instead of just owning the funnels that bring patients to them. Care coordination and navigation under AH ensures that members know about their options and benefit from the best providers with no cost to the member in most cases.

Aspirational healthcare is customizable to fit the specific goals and needs of your company. For larger companies, I recommend a self-insured plan along with subscription-based primary care and services to coordinate all levels of care. While you can build something like this yourself, Orriant offers easy access to all of these services.

For smaller companies, self-insurance likely won't make sense. Instead, we recommend you give employees money to spend on a program they want to use, which may be insurance, or it could be a sharing program or something else.

All of this will be covered in much more detail in the upcoming chapters. You'll learn exactly how to do it successfully, whether you're implementing a self-insured plan or enabling your employees to customize their own plans from scratch.

A NEW FRONT DOOR TO HEALTHCARE

Aligning your business objectives with your healthcare benefit offering is a fairly simple change to make, but it is the fundamental step to completely transforming healthcare. It's the first step in implementing aspirational healthcare. In fact, many large employers are rolling out a whole new form of healthcare by offering a subscription-based advanced primary care option that functions as their employees' front door to all of their healthcare needs.

In fact, I believe that the examples being set by large employers like Prudential Financial, Linde, Pitney Bowes, EY (Ernst & Young), and many other very large employers—who are all offering to pay 100% of costs for their employees to have access to this new form of primary care—are starting the biggest transformation in the healthcare industry to happen in the past 75 years. My hat is off to these innovative companies and all other employers who have begun funding this new front door.

Advanced primary care: A subscription-based model of primary care where a patient has a direct relationship with their provider and access to their care whenever they need it. Services are often delivered virtually or in the patient's home.

How does advanced primary care work?

You may be familiar with the concept of "concierge" or "retainer" medicine—it's been around for a long time. Basically, you pay your doctor a little additional money beyond or outside your insurance to have access to them whenever you need it. Membership-based *advanced primary care*, sometimes called direct primary care, is similar but does not bill insurance. In this model, healthcare providers charge a monthly fee to their patients rather than billing insurance. The monthly subscription covers all primary care. This allows primary care providers to avoid spending time and money on fighting with insurance in order to authorize treatments and get paid, and instead just focus on taking care of their patients.

One of the first doctors to adopt this model in Utah often spent six hours on their first visit with every patient—can you imagine what you'd talk to your doctor about for six hours? He wanted to know everything about his patients, from their career goals to their family and health history.

A doctor who uses this model can be more than just your doctor—they can be your partner to help you reach your dreams, there to support you through everything.

Now many large employers are supporting this system by offering to pay for direct primary care membership for their employees. They don't force their employees to use it, but they incentivize them to do so because it reduces the total cost of healthcare by reducing the number of hospitalizations while providing better care and creating happier employees.

Aspirational healthcare encourages the use of this subscription-based advanced primary care or direct primary care (DPC) as the front door to healthcare. We will go into more detail about this new front door to healthcare in chapter 7. It's a model that coordinates primary care and stays involved to coordinate care at all levels. And the results are remarkable.

CHAPTER 3

Elevate Your Business

If you're not making any intentional decisions about the healthcare you offer your employees, you're sliding backward.

Healthcare costs rise every year, often by leaps and bounds, and the quality of care provided isn't rising along with the costs.

The unfortunate truth is that the healthcare industry is set up to take advantage of businesses and their employees—the customers of the healthcare industry—in order to profit.

In the first chapter, we discussed the importance of identifying your business objectives related to healthcare and measuring to ensure they're being met. This is a concept that branches from Edwards Deming's principles.

Edwards Deming took the scientific method and converted it into an organization structure for continuous quality improvement.

Much of his process can be boiled down to asking these questions:

- Who is the customer?

- What will delight the customer?

- What process has the most impact in delighting the customer?

Monitor these processes closely and get those who are closest to the processes to find ways to improve them.

WHAT I LEARNED FROM RUNNING HOSPITALS THAT CEOS NEED TO KNOW

Understanding these principles and how they could—and should—be applied to healthcare is part of what ultimately led me out of my career as a hospital administrator.

The third hospital I helped run and the first job I took after I graduated with my MHA was in Rancho Bernardo, north of San Diego. The company I worked for had a very for-profit mindset, and they began asking me to do some things that made me uncomfortable, ethically speaking. So, I called my mentor, the administrator who had connected me with my first few jobs as CFO and had gone to work for Hospital Corporation of America in Houston. I told him I wasn't comfortable with the ethics of my company. I said to him, "Tell me about HCA—do you like working for them?" He said he did and offered to get me an interview in Nashville. HCA opened up a position for me in Texas as an assistant administrator. I loved working for the administrator there.

After running a couple more hospitals in Texas, my next job was opening a psychiatric hospital on a medical campus in Aiken, South Carolina, a well-to-do area surrounded by mansions and plantations. During my career running hospitals, I became an expert in helping hospitals become Joint Commission Accredited with Commendation. The Joint Commission is the accreditation organization for healthcare that hospitals bow to. As long as they're accredited with the Joint Commission, the large insurance companies will accept them and they don't need a separate certification to bill Medicare or Medicaid.

The Joint Commission had started implementing the Edwards Deming philosophies of continuous quality improvement (CQI). The Joint Commission decided to begin measuring the outcomes from the hospitals rather than simply ensuring they were following specific procedures, and I liked that idea.

What does it mean to measure outcomes instead of procedures? Well, if you ran a bakery, rather than just reviewing all the recipes, testing the oven temperature, timing how long it takes the bread to rise, and quizzing all the bakers on procedures, you might also taste the bread to see how good it is. While all the procedures are important, they don't make a difference if they don't create good outcomes, and the same applies to healthcare. Of course, we want providers to follow procedures and best practices, but healthcare has a human element, and what ultimately matters is the outcomes—the health of the patients, their satisfaction, and the costs.

It became very apparent to me that those same principles could be applied to the entire healthcare industry, starting by identifying the customer. Who is the customer? The one paying for healthcare—business leaders. Their employees are also customers because their outcomes are what will be measured, and they are the users of the benefits. There was nothing about my job that prioritized what business leaders or their employees wanted. It was just the opposite.

I saw that lack of alignment firsthand. Many of the problems in the healthcare industry are even worse in psychiatric care, where I was working. If you have a broken ankle, you can take an X-ray. But psychiatric care is very subjective. If the psychiatrist says you're sick, you're sick. And if psychiatrists have for-profit incentives to fill up the hospital beds, they're likely to just bring anyone in and have them stay exactly the amount of time the insurance company says they should.

Looking for ways to make the psychiatric hospital where I worked in Aiken more effective, I soon realized there was no need to run it as a hospital at all—it could be run simply as a department, and that would be better for the outcomes of the company. So, I made the recommendation to eliminate a number of jobs, including my own, in order to cut the costs of the administrative team.

The CEO of HCA heard about this, so he helped get me a job to be the COO of their largest psychiatric hospital in HCA, which was in Chicago. I went to work in Chicago, and during that time I said to my wife, "This industry, as a whole, is not living within my ethics. I don't think I can run hospitals anymore." I made a lot of money doing it, but I couldn't do it anymore.

Two men in Utah, Brent Hale and Ross Van Vranken, had come up with an idea to build a mental health benefits company where the focus was on managing healthcare by focusing on prevention. I interviewed with them and was fascinated with what they wanted to do: provide a new model of healthcare focused on taking care of people early before they ever have to go to the hospital. By designing the system around prevention rather than getting paid for the number of people we put in the hospital, we thought we could drive down the cost.

I came to Utah to be part of that company, Behavioral Health Strategies. As we began to put together a business plan, Brent and I asked, "Why do you have to be diagnosed with a mental illness to have someone in your corner to be a coach and supporter?"

We wanted to create a new level of healthcare—one based on coaching people. One of our objectives was to create a service that provided people with a coach to support them in reaching their goals in life. We set up a relationship with an insurance company to provide health coaching for the population with the highest number of claims every year, who spend a lot of money within the system and seldom get better.

Usually, about 5% of the population spends a large proportion of the healthcare cost. Insurance only works because a very small percentage of people use it, usually cancer cases and other illnesses that are expensive to treat. But there's also a group of people, about 1% of the population, who just don't recover—they continue to spend a large amount every year. They're people who get their sense of self-worth or security through the healthcare system and sometimes are labeled hypochondriacs. Their world revolves around their illnesses.

Doctors tend to get frustrated with these patients because they won't do anything—because they don't want to get better or because they don't believe their ailments will go away. Some of the most common illnesses these people suffer from are depression, diabetes, back problems, chronic fatigue, and stomach problems.

We told the insurance company to give us their most difficult patients and we'd give them a coach who would call or go to their homes a few times a week, giving them so much attention they wouldn't need to go see a doctor for attention. We identified these members by sorting those who had the highest number of claims consistently over a five-year period and were consistently spending a lot of money each of those five years The coaches helped them build their self-esteem and belief in their own ability to change their health. We promised that if at the end of the year we hadn't saved them money, we'd give the insurance companies their money back.

That first year, we treated about 15-20 patients and started sending a coach to their homes. We began helping people set up and track their goals. And it worked remarkably well. The coaches built relationships with these people and helped them improve their health by focusing on their life goals and what was important to them. And it saved the insurance company a great deal of money because these individuals had cost the plan significantly over the past five or more years.

Eventually, we split the company into two separate companies. The new company started out as Health Behavior Innovations and we eventually changed the name to Orriant, which is based on the Latin root words meaning "to rise up and be happy." Now Orriant offers a variety of services with that goal in mind. We've helped many companies implement aspirational healthcare and have seen tremendous results for employers and their employees.

ASPIRATIONAL HEALTHCARE CUTS COSTS

In chapter 1, we covered the four main ways that the healthcare system extracts excessive money from employers, but let's take a closer look at how that plays out in terms of health benefits.

The average annual cost of traditional insurance for employers is $14,000 per employee—and that's not counting the portion of the premium that the employee pays, which is often a fairly significant dent in their paycheck. That's an astronomical cost considering that the majority of people only use their insurance a few times a year for their annual exam and occasional doctor's visits.

Many companies that use an aspirational healthcare model spend half as much on employee healthcare.

The costs vary because each employer implements it differently, but we typically see a 40-60% reduction in costs, and some no longer charge their employees anything for their health benefits. Not only is it saving them money, but no-cost health coverage is a significantly attractive benefit to employees.

Despite companies and their employees paying large sums for health insurance every year, many individuals who have health insurance are still hesitant to see a doctor any more than strictly necessary, often when a problem has reached a point that it's no longer able to be ignored or managed without intervention. Costs to patients can still be high even after insurance, and the quality of care they receive often fails to help them reach their health goals.

As a patient, you're likely to spend several hundred dollars a month contributing to your insurance premium, and when you go to a provider to address your health concern, you may only get 10 or 15 minutes of their time before they write you a prescription or refer you to a specialist. They don't take the time to get to the root of your problem or help you find the right treatment plan for you, and you may walk away simply feeling frustrated after paying a copay or co-insurance out of pocket. If you need a procedure, that cost out of pocket can quickly become prohibitively expensive for many people.

As a result, healthcare fails to keep people healthy. Patients avoid using their insurance until absolutely necessary, and the majority of people who don't need any type of intensive treatment have no support from the healthcare system to maintain their health despite paying large sums of money to insurance every year.

Clearly, this insurance model has failed both employers and employees. The cost savings of the aspirational healthcare model go beyond just the cost of insurance—it provides a return in improved health, the value of which is unmatched.

Not only do healthier people save more on healthcare in the long run, but they are also happier and more productive, which is of high value not only to those individuals but also to their employers. Healthier individuals have better physical and mental capabilities, which they bring with them to work, resulting in increased productivity, morale, and quality of work.

Most CEOs I speak with agree that this is the ultimate goal of providing healthcare to their employees—they want a happy, healthy workforce. Not only will that workforce be more productive and perform at a higher level, but they'll also be easier to retain if they're happy with the healthcare they receive.

How does the aspirational healthcare model manage to save so much money?

ALIGN THE INTERESTS OF YOUR TEAM

Previously, we discussed the importance of alignment of interests in order to create effective, affordable healthcare. We've already established that there's a phenomenal amount of waste in the healthcare system. Of the $4.5 trillion dollars the U.S. spends on healthcare annually, only 27% goes to pay healthcare providers. Where does the other 73% go?

It goes into fighting with insurance companies and broker incentives. And it goes toward inflated costs driven by insurance companies and providers who know they can charge $72,000 for a procedure that only costs them $5,000. It goes toward all the waste in the system, including fraud and abuse.

That waste is caused by the people running these systems whose interests are to make money at every possible opportunity, robbing both patients and their employers.

Fraud in Healthcare

Unfortunately, fraud is entirely too common within the U.S. healthcare system and accounts for a significant amount of waste in healthcare spending. In his book *Never Pay the First Bill*, author Marshall Allan reveals the shocking data on just how prevalent fraud is and how little insurance companies do to prevent it. And their lack of responsibility in investigating fraud has led to employers and individuals paying the additional cost.

According to Allan, most experts put the total fraud within the healthcare system at about 10% of the total spend, meaning about $300-400 billion a year stolen from the healthcare system.

Fraud takes the form of profiteering and price gouging meant to exploit people's illnesses for money, but it doesn't stop there. Surprise billing is a common occurrence. One of the most prevalent forms of fraud is called upcoding, which is when a provider codes an office visit as a higher level of service than what was actually needed, allowing them to charge more.

Often, individuals facing the results of this fraud are left to fend for themselves with little to no support from their insurance providers. With one in six Americans in collections for medical debt, the costs are high and the consequences quite dire.

Allan argues, "As individuals and as employers, we need to defend ourselves from the system that is preying on us. Or we might even need to go on offense in some cases and take the fight to the system." I'd add that as employers, we have the power to fight against the system on behalf of ourselves and our employees.

One of the big secrets of the health insurance industry is that most brokers work for a big brokerage house. In these big houses, commissions are the primary source of revenue. With few exceptions, brokerage houses receive large overrides at the end of the year from insurance companies, which are for keeping a certain percentage of their business with the insurance company. Brokers who find better options to offer their clients are constrained by their own brokerage houses because they are dependent on those overrides, which can represent as much as 40% of the total revenue the brokerage house receives every year.

The majority of brokers don't have the ability to choose what's best for their clients because their employers, the brokerage houses, won't let them. They're only allowed to sell the BUCAs: Blue Cross, United, Cigna, or Aetna. Generally, the only brokers who have the freedom to do what's best for the client are those who work independently.

Seek out a benefits advisor who is CAA certified—a certified aspirational healthcare advisor is committed to aligning their compensation with the success of the company. If your advisor is not CAA certified, insist that they become certified or find a new advisor who is.

The next step to creating alignment is to change the way you and your employees interact with healthcare by changing the front door—how they enter the healthcare system.

CHANGE THE FRONT DOOR TO HEALTHCARE

When an employer hands their employees an insurance policy, it comes with a network. If the employee goes to any of the providers within that network, they pay a lower deductible and copay.

If you have a traditional insurance policy, when you need to see a doctor, you go to the network list. But almost all of those doctors are paid by hospitals and are being held accountable to reach a certain number of relative value units (RVUs) every day. RVUs include items like patient visits, procedures, and tests. You get to spend 10 minutes with the doctor and will walk out with either a prescription or a referral to a specialist, who is likely within that hospital network.

The front door to healthcare is primary care, and many of those primary care physicians are being held accountable to maintain a certain level of RVUs every day by the hospitals that own them. The hospitals want them to send people to see their specialists, use their MRI machines, take tests at their testing centers, and more. People are being herded through the system like cattle. Physicians don't often take the time to get to know the patient or find out what the real problem is and what each individual needs.

Primary care physicians need to be separated from hospitals and the hospitals' revenue goals.

By changing the front door to healthcare, we can stop herding people into hospitals. That's what the Nuka System did—they created a massively powerful primary care system based on relationships and focused on serving customers. And now we're doing the same thing through aspirational healthcare, creating a network across the country of independent providers who can be easily accessed through a simple system that employers can provide to their employees. The hard work has already been done to make it possible to offer subscription-based advanced primary care.

Subscription-based advanced primary care will be a more expensive form of primary care, but can drive down your total cost of healthcare by as much as half of the cost of traditional healthcare. Furthermore, it will save money for your employees in the form of premiums, copays, and co-insurance. It does this by providing a much higher level of primary care where the provider can practice at the top of their license and focus on enhancing health and not just treating symptoms.

When primary care providers aren't beholden to hospitals, they're able to provide better care—and total healthcare costs are far less expensive because of savings from lowering the cost of secondary care such as specialists, imaging, and hospitalizations. We'll go into more detail about subscription-based advanced primary care in chapter 7.

CHOOSE THE BEST PROVIDERS

If you have a traditional insurance plan and you need knee surgery such as an ACL repair, that insurance company has a network of providers with whom they're contracted, and they'll require you to use one of those providers in order to receive your full benefit. Let's say they're contracted with a hospital that charges $72,000 for an ACL repair and gets a three-star rating, and they're also contracted with a hospital that does that same surgery for $7,000 and gets a five-star rating. Nobody within the insurance system is going to steer you toward the higher-rated, lower-cost option.

Why would the insurance company want to pay more for a lower-quality service? When you understand the way insurance companies work, it makes sense. They make more money for their shareholders when the costs of healthcare increase. Insurance companies make projections that they need to hit in order to increase their profits, and those projections grow 10-20% every year to give their shareholders better returns. It's not about saving money—they don't make as much profit when they save money.

Insurance companies have all sorts of tricks they use to hit their projections, and one of those is the process of pre-authorization. For many procedures, insurance companies require pre-authorization before they agree to pay, and this requires hospitals to submit a request for approval before they bill the insurance. An extra step and more time increase the cost of billing.

During the COVID-19 pandemic when elective surgeries— which produce the biggest profits—decreased significantly, some insurance companies began approving many more procedures to hit their projections. However, when the pandemic slowed down, they restricted approvals to keep costs in line with their projections, making it more difficult to get an elective surgery approved. You can see how they work the system to their advantage in order to create the highest profits. (This was shared with me by someone who had been an underwriter for one of the big insurance companies.)

Aspirational healthcare is able to access better healthcare for a lower price by working directly with healthcare providers. You can save money by choosing lower-cost and higher-rated providers who have been shown to produce good health outcomes. Better health outcomes save money in the long run by reducing the need for additional care. All of this is possible as a result of healthcare cost transparency data, which we'll discuss more in chapter 8.

When you cut out the middlemen and work directly with healthcare providers, you can also leverage the power of cash to take advantage of cash discounts, which often lower costs significantly more. We'll cover more on the *power of cash* in chapter 8.

BYPASS EXCESSIVE DRUG PROFITS

Prescription drugs are another major cost of healthcare, and the price that individuals and employers pay is often well above what the actual costs should be. But it's not for the reasons many people tend to think—much of it is due to a type of company many people aren't even aware exists: pharmacy benefit managers (PBMs).

A PBM operates somewhat like insurance in that they play the middlemen between drug manufacturers and patients purchasing prescriptions at pharmacies. PBMs are contracted with insurance providers and with employers to help them reduce the costs of prescriptions, but in effect, they only drive costs up.

Three large PBMs represent the vast majority of the industry, and so they have an enormous amount of control over the costs of drugs. While it may appear that they're saving their clients' money, it's often as a result of huge markups those very PBMs are responsible for. A *New York Times* article,[7] "The Opaque Industry Secretly Inflating Prices for Prescription Drugs," revealed how PBMs actually increase costs rather than reducing them. They make much of their money through hidden markups, which are often egregious.

For employers with self-funded plans, contracting with a large PBM seems to make sense because they receive rebates from the PBM. It may seem like those rebates are helping them fund their healthcare plans, but that money is already accounted for in the costs of the drugs.

I always recommend that employers don't use those large PBMs and instead look for a PBM that's transparent about their pricing. The best way to ensure transparency is to spell out the end-user cost of every drug in your contract with the PBM and then leverage market forces to get the best price. This way, the PBM can't work their magic formulas to strip profits out of the system. We'll cover more about bypassing excessive drug profits in chapter 9, but much of it comes down to simply choosing a PBM that's transparent in their profits and willing to list every drug price in their contract.

ENCOURAGE HEALTHIER CHOICES

One of the most effective ways to reduce healthcare spending is simply to improve our individual health choices. In fact, 87.5% of healthcare spend can be traced back to a person's choice.

Very few health problems are the result of genetics
or accidents alone. The vast majority are caused simply by
the way people take care of their own health.

Of course, a healthcare system with a priority of making money doesn't want to address this issue. But the matter is more complicated than just that. After all, the biggest challenge healthcare providers face is getting people to change their behavior. It's easier to take someone's heart out and replace it than it is to get them to change their behavior.

It was this very problem that I wanted to address when I left hospital administration. How can you get people to change their behavior? The answer is through coaching, but not just any kind of coaching.

Daniel Pink is one of my favorite behavioralist speakers and he described a simple, effective strategy: "People will do simple tasks for rewards." You can get people to do almost any simple task by giving them a big enough reward, but rewards are very ineffective at getting people to make long-term behavioral changes.

For example, think of the show *The Biggest Loser.* The weight loss those people experienced on that show was amazing—but almost every contestant put it all back on and more, which I believe was one of the reasons it finally went off the air. Why would someone who just went from 300 pounds to 160 put it all back on? Because the environment the show created offered amazing rewards for a task but didn't address long-term behavior change.

So how do you get people to change their behavior? You work with a coach who builds a genuine relationship with you. Someone who cares. A coach asks, "What do *you* want?" It's not about what the coach, the doctor, the healthcare system, or the employer want—it's about what the individual wants.

The approach of the traditional healthcare system is asking people to comply with a set of recommendations to better manage their health. But healthcare should take the opposite approach by focusing on helping people do what they want to do. People are far more likely to improve their lifestyles when it is a part of reaching their aspirations.

You can focus your benefits strategy around supporting your employees in reaching their personal aspirations, which will encourage healthier lifestyle choices and promote behavioral change. We'll discuss how to do this in more detail in the coming chapters.

HOW ONE COMPANY DROPPED COSTS BY 50%

Greg Kaupp, CEO of ArcherPoint, managed to halve the cost of healthcare for his employees through a self-funded aspirational healthcare plan while improving employee health benefits, reducing costs to employees, and offering more benefits than they previously had. They followed many of the aspirational healthcare strategies to create a system that worked for their company.

I had the opportunity to hear Darrell present at my Vistage group back in January 2019. Like most of my peer group, we had been facing rising healthcare costs every year since we started our business in 2002. We were faced every year with a decision either to deal with the rising costs or reduce benefits. After nearly 17 years of spiraling costs, we knew that there would come a day in the not-too-distant future when the business and our employees wouldn't be able to maintain the level of healthcare that we currently provided.

Based on Darrell's insights, we began to dive into what it would look like for an organization of hundreds to go self-funded.

The response I got from the organization was predictable—it was too risky and not worth doing. However, I challenged our organization to come up with an alternative to what Darrell proposed to address the rising cost of healthcare for our organization. None of them had any answers.

Darrell connected us with a broker who specializes in the type of self-insurance plans that Darrell proposed. After a lot of hand-wringing and due diligence, we decided to take the plunge. Of our 100 employees, roughly half opted for our self-funded insurance, with the other half obtaining coverage through their spouses. That meant we had about 50 on the plan.

After our first year, we cut our health insurance costs in half. We decided for year two that we had enough confidence in our plan that we reduced the employee contribution to health insurance premiums by 25%, saving costs for our employees. We also added an additional health and wellness benefit for all employees, including those not currently on the health insurance plan. The final piece was that we wanted to add something to our plan that made it truly unique, so we added a therapeutic massage benefit.

There was a lot of good that came out of our switch to self-insurance. However, it is important to go into the process with your eyes wide open. To achieve significant savings requires employees to become much more involved in the medical billing process, which is why we've now partnered with Orriant to take care of the problem.

Over time, we have made improvements to our plan to increase employee satisfaction. We have found that we needed to make changes to our network strategy. We believe that the tremendous savings and increased benefits are well worth the challenges of switching to a self-insured plan. The key is to work with a broker, third-party administrator, and a claims advocate who truly understand how to make all this work together for the benefit of the organization and its employees.

Misunderstandings About Aspirational Healthcare

How can I ask my employees to make such a big change?

Remember that choice is one of the key principles of aspirational healthcare. You don't have to force any changes. In fact, the aspirational healthcare model offers more options to your employees than they previously had. The change will come by providing incentives for them to switch to something better.

For more information on helping employees through the transition, see chapters 5 and 12.

CHAPTER 4

Relationships Make Healthcare Better

Aspirational healthcare is fundamentally different from any other healthcare system—a system that redefines healthcare to focus around the principles of alignment of interests, choice, and relationship. To make this system successful, we have to think about healthcare entirely differently.

> Healthcare can be much more than just the place you go when you break—it can be a guest at your table, a cheerleader in your corner. Whatever you're trying to reach in life, healthcare can be your partner in helping you reach it.

How would it feel if the person behind the white coat was someone you knew and trusted?

Imagine being able to call your doctor on their cell at any time when you have a concern. Imagine having your physician visit you in your home, take the time to get to know you, and follow up with you regularly. Imagine having a coach in your corner to help you achieve your goals, whether they're health related or not!

Healthcare can encompass so much more than just caring for your body; it's about your total well-being. And the current system doesn't take into account all of the other aspects of life that impact your optimal health. Aspirational healthcare does.

I often ask people to define what health means to them. The concept of health isn't a single thing. There's no particular set of traits we can point to as "healthy" or "unhealthy," and health exists on many spectrums. But I have found one definition that most people find satisfactory—the answer that continues to bubble to the surface.

Being healthy means being able to do what you want to do.

So the role of healthcare, in that case, is to support our ability to do what we want to do. What's necessary in order to create a system that can achieve this is relationships.

REDEFINING HEALTHCARE

Healthcare in the U.S. is mostly science-based and involves very little relationship. In other words, the system is built around diagnoses and treatment plans.

When my mom had a stroke, a team came in and put her through assessments involving a variety of questions and recorded everything. Everything they did was to meet required policies based on evidence-based practices. Some of those people would spend some time getting to know my mom, but most of them did not.

In healthcare, relationships trump science. At Southcentral Foundation's Nuka Conference that takes place in June every year, attendees spend five days learning from one of the world's leading examples of healthcare redesign.

The Nuka System of Care is designed to create health and help people reach their dreams, and that happens through relationships. Three out of those five days, the attendees go through the same relationship-focused training that all employees, doctors, and nurses go through. The training is about how to create relationships and build trust with customer-owners (patients). They learn how to use appropriate communication to help patients feel safe enough to share their stories. Communication comes first because if you can get someone to share their story and you react appropriately, nothing builds relationships stronger and faster.

The reality is that when you have a strong relationship with your healthcare provider, it gives you a level of accountability and support to reach your goals that could never be accomplished through the transactional interactions in the traditional U.S. healthcare system.

But let's get one thing clear: healthcare should not just be about creating *compliance*. It's not about getting patients to follow through on what their doctors tell them to do. In fact, aspirational healthcare is about the opposite of that.

I went to Washington for a big healthcare innovation conference. The night before the conference started, I got to introduce the SCF President and CEO, April Kyle, and the Executive Vice President of Specialty Care Services, Dr. Eby, to the board of the conference. They joined us virtually. I asked the board members, "Why in the world would you think that an aspirational healthcare model like Nuka would spend three days teaching you how to build trusting relationships with people?"

Everyone had something to say, and they chattered on for a while. Then one person spoke up and said, "I think there's one very simple thing, which is people are more likely to comply with their therapy if they don't want to disappoint their provider." April Kyle responded, "I would turn that around and say healthcare can do better if we trust families and communities to know best what families need. . . . How do we do a good job listening to people and families and using their direction to build a healthcare system that complies with their needs? It's a play on where power sits, and trust and relationship are the way that you get to that."

Dr. Eby responded, "My personal tolerance for words that our employees and other people say is pretty big. We try not to use 'patient' anymore; we use 'customer-owner.' But the one that I don't tolerate is whenever anyone talks about patients being compliant. It's the other way around. How do we comply with their wants, needs, and wishes to support them on their journey? And to judge people as compliant or non-compliant because they followed or didn't follow what we in our professional and institutional arrogance told them to do is offensive and does harm and is abusive!"

> Healthcare is not about whether the patient is compliant with the doctor. It's about whether healthcare is compliant with the dreams, goals, and aspirations of the individuals, the families, and the communities it serves.

The very thought that people should come to healthcare to be compliant in order to take better care of their health is exactly what's wrong with healthcare. The Nuka System of Care was built around healthcare coming to members of its communities to help them reach their dreams, goals, and aspirations. The healthcare system doesn't get to dictate what people should be working toward.

I learned this lesson early on as I began to learn about aspirational healthcare, and it's why our coaches never lay out or force goals on people. Instead, they ask about the customers' goals and how they can support them. That support can and often does include health education as well as accountability, but it is personalized to the individual.

This mindset is vital to the success of aspirational healthcare. If your goal in providing healthcare to your employees is talent retention and having a healthy and productive workforce, you can't impose healthcare on your employees. Nobody wants to do something because they've been told to do it. But if you have the mindset of supporting people to help them develop in the ways they want and pursue their goals, that will change the way your employees approach healthcare and the choices they make.

Many people have become disenfranchised with the healthcare system because of the institutional arrogance that gets in the way of relationships. The assumption that the doctor knows what's best for the patient doesn't allow people agency in their own healthcare journeys.

People want to be seen and known, and that's a prerequisite for any kind of relationship that will have any impact on your life. In the U.S. healthcare system, your primary healthcare physician simply doesn't have the time to spend with you in order to build a strong relationship. They don't have the time to educate you about your health, so you receive canned answers and treatment plans that aren't personalized to your particular needs. For example, if you're having digestive issues, you might be put on a highly restrictive diet that isn't sustainable for you long term, which ultimately sets you up to fail—especially if following the restrictive diet is more painful than your symptoms.

But if you have a strong relationship with your doctor and they understand your pain points, your priorities, and your goals, you can work together to develop customized solutions to help you create better health outcomes that match your desires.

Nuka created a relationship-based system with the goal that your care team would become part of your path to wellness, someone to guide you on your journey and be there when you need them. They wanted your doctor, the front door into healthcare, to be someone who knows you and your family and will spend the time necessary to find a solution that meets your needs, rather than just doing the best they can within the 10 minutes they're allotted for your appointment.

IMPROVING HEALTH THROUGH COACHING

Improving health is often about changing behavior, and making long-term changes to your behavior is hard. Understanding the stages a person goes through in enacting change helps us understand what's needed in order to move from one stage to the next.

James Prochaska's transtheoretical model of change lays out five stages of change:

1. Precontemplation – No awareness that a change is needed

2. Contemplation – Awareness that a change is needed but no plans exist to take action on the change

3. Determination/preparation – Planning to take action on a change within the next month

4. Action – Behavior changed within the last six months, risk of relapse to earlier stages is still high

5. Maintenance – Behavior change has been sustained for more than six months without relapse to previous stages

While the transtheoretical model of change has become quite popular and well recognized, many people miss one of the most important aspects of the entire study.

Prochaska's research underscores that social support can significantly impact an individual's ability to progress through the stages of change by providing encouragement, accountability, and practical assistance.

What we see in behavior changes regarding health is that without a coach, people in good health tend to migrate toward worse health, while people in poor health who do have a coach migrate toward better health.

In partnership with Brigham Young University, Orriant produced a study[8] to determine the effectiveness of health coaching. A professor put the time and effort into gathering data from four of our major clients and published an international study that mapped the overall improvement statistics over three years. The study concluded, "Participants had fewer healthcare claims and lower costs than nonparticipants, which became more pronounced over the study period. Health risks and PWP (personal wellness profile) results significantly improved, more so in those in poorer health at baseline who worked with a health coach. Mean difference between health age and potential achievable age significantly decreased, more so for men than women and among those with the greatest need for improvement."

Later, we took all of our 80 clients at the time and produced a white paper showing the statistics for all of them in order to demonstrate the integrity of our results. We wanted to show that the outcomes were excellent with every one of our clients, and we didn't just pick our favorite four clients with the best results.

The data reported in the white paper showed that the principles of choice and relationship are intrinsically linked.

You cannot force a relationship onto someone, so as an employer you must recognize that you're simply offering options and incentives to encourage relationships. You cannot tell your employees they must take part in something, or they will assume it's for your benefit and not for theirs. Nobody wants to be forced to do anything, and if they are forced, they're going to resent it.

HARNESSING THE POWER OF STORYTELLING IN HEALTHCARE

Nuka has so thoroughly built storytelling into their healthcare system that every employee is required to go through a three-day training program on effective communication skills. They learn to build trust with customers to encourage the sharing of stories and respond to those stories respectfully: When someone has shared their story with you, the first thing you should do is thank them for being willing to share. Encouraging people to share their story gives them an opportunity to build trust with you.

It's important that the individual is the one to tell their own story—how they got to where they are and what their life experiences have been. Not only does this establish trust, but it gives the provider information to partner with and guide each customer to their desired destinations.

At Orriant, we've found storytelling to be a particularly important tool in our coaching services. As part of the aspirational healthcare model, it's a coach's job to partner with the patient to meet their goals, and storytelling plays a vital role in that. It's easy for a healthcare professional to steer the conversation with a customer, and they may even have an agenda of what they'd like to accomplish with that customer. But it's important that the patient's voice is reflected in every conversation; even if the coach is driving the conversation, the person should be the one in control.

The coach is simply there to create a space in the person's life where they can look at their own health and well-being, understand where they are, and determine where they want to be. From there, the coach can help them find a path that works for them to reach their desired destination. By just creating a space for someone to examine their own health and well-being, it's remarkable what can happen.

The traditional model of healthcare tells people to stop and manage their bodies better. Aspirational healthcare doesn't do that—instead, it asks healthcare professionals to jump on board, find out what a person's destination is, and use their expertise to help them reach it. Often, people aren't even thinking about their destinations, and having a professional to help them move toward their aspirations can take them much further than they'd have dreamed.

Dr. Eby of SCF told a story about one of his patients, a grandfather, that illustrates how storytelling plays a vital role in healthcare.

Dr. Eby needed to explain to this grandfather, an Alaska Native person, that his A1C levels were high, meaning he was prediabetic, and he needed to better manage those levels. But instead of taking the traditional approach, he connected it to this grandfather's story, who wanted to teach his grandkids how to hunt and fish and pick berries. Dr. Eby focused on the need to be careful about his finger-tips, because diabetes can numb the nerves on the end of his fingers, and he needs feeling in his fingers to tell if berries are ripe. He also explained that the nerves in his feet might be affected as well, and he needs to be able to feel his feet when hunting and fishing.

Healthcare is *not* about getting people to do what healthcare wants them to do—it's about partnering with people to help them do what *they* want to do.

Misunderstandings About Aspirational Healthcare

Is relationship-based healthcare helpful for everyone?

While some people only see their doctor once or twice a year (or even less frequently), everyone can benefit from relationship-based healthcare to help them reach their life aspirations. It's a model of whole-person healthcare that functions differently from traditional healthcare and extends much further than just treating illnesses.

If you find anybody whose dad is a doctor and ask them about their experience growing up in healthcare, they'll tell you they just went to their dad anytime they needed something. We're trying to create that kind of a relationship for everybody, so that engaging in the healthcare system is like calling your dad. If your healthcare provider was a member of your family, you would be more apt to address issues quickly and ask questions whenever you wanted.

Of course, you can't force people into relationships—it has to be their choice to engage. As with every aspect of aspirational healthcare, choice remains one of the top priorities.

CHAPTER 5

The Value of a Healthy Workforce

Most CEOs I've spoken to about healthcare agree that employee well-being is one of their top business objectives in purchasing healthcare, and for good reason: employees who are healthy, happy, and satisfied with their healthcare are not only more effective at their jobs but are also more likely to stay with the company long term—especially if a job change means losing their highly valued and unique health benefits and their relationships with their healthcare providers.

However, most CEOs will say, "I have a wellness program, so I am already addressing my employees' well-being." I have a few things to say about the wellness industry in the U.S. Corporations waste billions of dollars every year on wellness programs that are based on bad science. The vast majority of wellness programs do little more than hand out incentives for doing simple tasks. The idea that you can accomplish the hardest thing there is to do in healthcare—help people change lifestyles and behaviors—through these types of wellness programs is ludicrous.

These wellness programs make profits and employers see little impact on the overall health of their employees. People tell me all the time that they participate in their company's wellness program so they can earn their incentives but agree that it has done nothing to change their overall health. Pull the plug on these kinds of wellness programs and stop wasting your money.

The foundation of your wellness program should be to encourage the vast majority of your members to have a relationship with a personal success coach. A long-term relationship with a coach who supports people in reaching their own goals and aspirations is the only strategy that has been shown to have real impact on population health improvement. If you want to reward your employees for a task, reward them for engaging in a relationship with a coach. The reward won't change their behavior, but their relationship with a coach can. I covered this in chapter 3.

Andy Crighton, M.D., who was the chief medical officer for Prudential Financial, wrote a case study about their company's decision to prioritize the well-being of their employees. In it, he wrote, "When the Affordable Care Act became law in 2010, the Health and Wellness leadership team stepped back to evaluate whether or not health would still be important for the company if Prudential was not paying directly for medical insurance. Prudential's international presence, with about 20,000 employees in Japan, gave them experience with this model of healthcare. As a result, they ultimately decided health and performance would still be crucial to keep Prudential competitive. This led to the team adopting the broader aspects of health and well-being: physical, emotional, social, spiritual, and financial."

In other words, Prudential Financial determined that even if their company was not required to provide healthcare for their employees, they would still do so because the health and well-being of their workforce was important to them. And they're not alone in that sentiment.

It's no wonder that employers want a healthy workforce. Employee health and satisfaction plays a significant role in productivity and quality of work, and while there's plenty of data to back that up, this makes sense on a very intuitive level. On a day when you're not feeling well, whether because of a physical or mental ailment, you're simply not able to get as much done as on a day when you're feeling mentally and physically strong. Not only are symptoms of poor health a hindrance to your work performance, but illness within your family can play a major role in your mental health and cause distraction. Even the financial stress of medical bills can create negative effects on productivity and quality of work.

Think about it this way: On days when you achieve something you're proud of or manage to surpass your productivity goals, what do you feel like? Probably you feel alert, focused, physically sound, and emotionally well—maybe even content or happy. Feeling well actually contributes to your effectiveness.

Employee well-being is about more than just physical health. It's about morale. And the best CEOs understand the importance of morale not just on an individual level but also as a key to effective teamwork. An employee with poor morale—which is often connected to their sense of well-being—can quickly drag down the morale of the rest of the team. On the flip side, high morale can also be contagious. And a workforce with a strong sense of well-being, who trusts that you care about their interests, will be willing to go much further than one who suspects they only matter to you insofar as they make you money.

In order to improve employee well-being, you must move past the mindset that healthcare is just a requirement, a cost of doing business and nothing more. If you truly believe that, your employees will too, and it will erode their trust in you.

Imagine saying to your employees, "I wouldn't pay to keep you healthy if I didn't have to." Would you want to work for someone with that mindset? Probably not. In fact, you'd likely resent them, and you certainly wouldn't give them your best work. But if you instead said to your employees, "I care about your well-being and your family, and I want to take care of you by providing the best available healthcare options so you can choose what works for you," that would create a much different reaction.

Aspirational healthcare allows you to have the best of both worlds—saving money on healthcare costs while providing a whole new level of healthcare to keep your employees healthy and happy.

FOCUSING HEALTHCARE ON THE WHOLE PERSON

By now, you've gotten an idea of how aspirational healthcare is beneficial to health outcomes. You understand the benefits of relationship-based healthcare in helping people make healthier lifestyle choices and changing their behavior through coaching. But I want to dig a little bit deeper.

Aspirational healthcare is designed around the whole person in order to maximize its effectiveness and create the best outcomes. It goes much further than the traditional American healthcare approach of treating illnesses and also further than simply applying preventive medicine. Instead, it acknowledges the differences in every person and the various factors at play in their lives that influence health from a variety of angles.

For example, take mental health. In the U.S., there's a common cultural idea that physical health and mental health are two separate realms, and while we may acknowledge that they affect one another, we ultimately tend to treat them separately. But these two aspects of health are inseparably linked and are often influenced by a variety of outside factors that a doctor may not consider. After all, they don't have time to unravel all of the aspects of someone's life that may be influencing their health, so they're trained to give standard advice, prescriptions, and referrals for certain conditions.

With relationship-based healthcare, your doctor can take the time to learn about your lifestyle, your habits, your dreams and goals, and parts of your past that have shaped you. They can take all of these things and more into account and work with you to develop solutions that address root causes of problems and that enable you to follow through. In addition, you will have a coach to help you stay accountable to reach your goals.

The most effective treatment for anything is the treatment you can follow through on. Often, treatment must go beyond what a pill or a procedure can provide in order to be effective.

Our lifestyles and our bodies are complex systems that interact and influence each other in ways we don't always expect. In the U.S. healthcare system, it may take significant persistence and patience in order to discover the root cause of a problem and find an effective treatment plan. If you haven't experienced this yourself, you likely know someone with a complicated health history who has been to doctor after doctor looking for answers, only to come up with few definitive answers and perhaps a myriad of pills (along with some significant medical bills).

Aspirational healthcare allows people to dive deep with their doctors and gives them someone who knows their entire story to help them navigate the larger healthcare system, if they need to see specialists or get other forms of treatment. This allows for a better integration of a variety of treatments to maximize health outcomes.

For example, someone with ADHD who is also struggling with health concerns such as high cholesterol or weight gain may need more than just advice on how to change their diet in order to succeed. They may need someone who specializes in ADHD to help them learn to build habits around better dietary choices while their coach helps to keep them on track with their goals.

> Aspirational healthcare allows for a multifaceted, in-depth approach to healthcare that treats the whole person by customizing treatment to their individual needs and desires.

HEALTHCARE PERSONALIZED TO YOUR GOALS

Healthcare focused around an individual's goals leads to better outcomes by tapping into what matters to that person. It's the ultimate form of personalized healthcare. And those goals don't have to be health related—whole-person healthcare means every aspect of a person's life, not just physical or even mental health.

If your goal is to own a home, that may require some behavioral changes in the way you manage your finances, which is likely to cause lifestyle changes as well—having a coach in your corner to support you as you navigate those changes can make the difference between healthy and unhealthy behaviors. If your goal is to run a marathon, that's going to require physical conditioning and some potential diet changes—your coach can help you develop new routines and keep you accountable. If your goal is to spend more time with your kids, in addition to adjusting your schedule, you may also need to become more physically fit in order to participate in the activities your kids want to do.

Achieving your goals is empowering and uplifting. It helps you believe in yourself and make healthier choices. And the reality is that most people's goals are aimed at a healthier life overall and are often tied to health. After all, what it means to be healthy is being able to do what you want to do with energy and vitality, unhindered by any aspect of your health.

Most individuals want to be healthy! They want to be able to do what they want to do, and so by serving those goals, aspirational healthcare can tap into their natural motivation in order to help them make healthier choices and positive behavioral changes.

THE VALUE OF CHOICE

As one of the three principles of aspirational healthcare, choice plays a significant role in the healthcare's success, and that role extends deeper than simply choosing the type of healthcare you want. In fact, it applies to every part of the healthcare process, which is a large part of what sets aspirational healthcare apart.

Why is choice so important? Because it allows individuals to use their judgment to pick what's best for them and their families, leading to better health outcomes. Even if you could force someone to participate in something they don't want to do, they wouldn't benefit from it in the same way as someone who chose to do it.

This principle is reflected in the structure of aspirational health-care, as patients are given choices in how they want to engage with healthcare—when, where, and to what extent. They're an active par-ticipant in creating treatment plans and steps to reach their goals. They choose what they want to work toward based on what is and isn't important to them.

Individuals are also given a choice when it comes to what pro-viders they can work with, often without the restrictions of an insur-ance network to limit their options.

Most importantly, people are more likely to succeed at goals they've set for themselves with a support system behind them. Choice gives people agency in their healthcare, something the tradi-tional U.S. healthcare system doesn't accomplish well.

FINANCIAL INCENTIVES AND BENEFITS

The well-being of your employees includes their financial well-being. Finances have a significant impact on well-being, from the level of healthcare someone is able to access to the stresses that come along with financial burden and even the lifestyle variations between dif-ferent income levels that impact a person's health. Financial well-being and physical and mental well-being are deeply linked.

Most of us know someone who has refused to go the doctor—or even the emergency room—when it was clear they needed to. If you've just cut open your hand, the cost of seeking care may sway you to just bandage it yourself, even if it's truly a wound that needs stitches. The same goes for health conditions that are less clearly an emergency—you may know your health is declining, but you don't want to navigate the difficult healthcare system and the cost of getting treatment is often unknown. These barriers may lead you to delay seeking care until it's too late for you to fully recover.

Aspirational healthcare directly addresses and prevents these problems by changing the front door to healthcare: primary care. You can contact your doctor at any time, and often it's as simple as sending a text message. And because you see your provider or members of their clinical team regularly, you're able to bring up any changes in your health as they happen, preventing much more costly treatments later on.

We'll go into more detail on how this system works in chapters 8 and 9, but for now, I want you to understand that ease of access to trusted doctors is essential to preventive care.

Not only do employees receive better healthcare, but they save money doing it. They don't pay high insurance premiums, copays, or co-insurance, so they never have to worry about the cost to them when they see their primary care doctor. The primary care provider receives a fixed monthly retainer to take care of the member. The only exception to this is those who choose to access their primary care through a high-deductible plan and use a health savings account (HSA) to pay. But in most of those cases, they are using money given to them by their employer.

When it comes to specialists, catastrophic care, and other larger expenses, employers have options about how to cover these costs. For larger companies, this is usually through a self-funded plan where the employee pays very little or even nothing, since the employer is able to access significantly discounted rates by leveraging the power of cash. We'll cover how this works in chapter 8.

For smaller companies, the strategies are more varied and customized, and the employee will have options for the kind of plan they use to cover medical costs. Employers have a variety of tools to help keep costs low and cover medical expenses, which are covered in chapters 8 and 9.

One example of these tools is a *health-sharing program*, a lower-cost option to pay for healthcare that works differently from health insurance. While health-sharing programs are not the best solution for every individual (because preexisting conditions are not shared initially), for the majority of people, they can be more cost-effective than insurance while paying for all or most of their health needs. I and many of my employees use health-sharing programs and have been extremely happy with them. We'll cover more on sharing programs in chapter 10.

Additionally, employees receive financial incentives from you, their employer, to use subscription-based primary care and health coaching because it benefits both of you—you both save money on healthcare and they have better health outcomes as a result.

For more information about how to set up financial incentives, see chapter 9.

AN EXAMPLE OF INDIVIDUALIZING HEALTHCARE

Amy, one of my employees, has had thousands of dollars of healthcare covered by her aspirational healthcare plan, which she's customized to work for her individual needs. Here is her story:

I haven't paid for healthcare in years. It's been fabulous and I feel fully supported for anything I need. One of my primary needs was infertility treatments, along with various women's issues. I don't have insurance—instead, I use a sharing program called Sedera.

Under that sharing program, like many other sharing programs, you create a need, which is a specific issue you're experiencing with your health. So I created an ambiguous need for simply "women's health." Over the past six years, under that one need, I've received between $30,000-50,000 worth of healthcare that hasn't been billed to me. That has included multiple visits with my OB as I went through years of infertility treatments, and while those treatments weren't paid for entirely by my sharing program, I was able to pay for them using the EBHRA (excepted benefit health reimbursement arrangement, covered in chapter 10) that Darrell gives me, which can go toward any healthcare needs. After years of infertility treatments, I had a full hysterectomy that was entirely paid for under the same need of "women's health."

Infertility is notoriously not well covered by health insurance, which is a total gap in the U.S. healthcare system. But I felt fully supported by my sharing network and the excess funds my employer gives me to disperse how I want. With a traditional insurance plan, I would have paid for most of that out of pocket.

What I learned is that I had to be much more invested in the entire healthcare program, getting codes, asking for good faith estimates, making phone calls to billing departments, and proactively asking for information. I had to be an active consumer. But because I did all of that, my sharing network approved all of it and cut me a check for $15,000 that went directly into my bank account so I could pay with my card the day I went in for surgery. I'm always very proactive in saying, "I'm cash pay. What discount are you giving me? I need the itemized receipt."

Misunderstandings About Aspirational Healthcare

What happens if an employee wants to keep their current doctor?

They have the choice to do so. If they currently have a great relationship with their doctor, they can stay with that doctor. They will likely have to pay copays and deductibles, but they should have that choice. Aspirational healthcare is structured to incentivize employees to utilize subscription-based primary care because, in most cases, they can have much quicker access to their primary care provider, who will often spend more time with them.

Is aspirational healthcare best for everyone?

Aspirational healthcare simply gives people more options. For some people, a traditional insurance plan may be the best option, and an aspirational healthcare strategy allows them to choose that. Choice is so important because your employees know their own situations best. For most employees, the new options offered will be better for them, but that won't be the case for all.

Each person must evaluate what's best for their family and their situation. Approaching healthcare benefits through an aspirational model simply refers to offering benefits in a way that your employees can use your benefit dollars to best meet their needs.

CHAPTER 6

Staying Competitive by Improving Employee Well-Being

If you're purchasing healthcare with the goal of attracting and retaining top talent, that benefit will go much farther if you offer a higher quality of healthcare than they can find elsewhere. Healthcare is one of the highest-value aspects of an employee's benefit package, and for good reason. Purchasing health insurance without employer or government assistance can be prohibitively expensive, so most Americans rely on their employers to provide this critical service. We all need healthcare and we all want better healthcare, and that can play a significant role in an employee's decision to stay with their employer or look for a new one.

As more businesses adopt the aspirational healthcare model, employees will have increased options for healthcare benefits as part of their benefits packages, and it will become all the more important for employers to offer excellent healthcare in order to compete.

The success of this model is clear. The Nuka System of Care has demonstrated its ability to revolutionize healthcare, and many organizations are beginning to follow in their steps.

Aspirational healthcare can be used by any size company. There are different ways of doing it based on business size, but every company can offer a healthcare system that puts more resources into helping people reach their goals and build relationships.

Every company can have dashboards that reflect how their investments in healthcare benefits are working to reach their goals.

We've been successful at convincing some of the largest employers in America to roll out an aspirational healthcare model, including Pitney Bowes, Prudential Financial, Linde, and EY. In fact, at the time of this writing, many of the largest employers in America, representing over 6 million employees, have rolled out or are rolling out this new model of healthcare by offering to pay for subscription-based direct primary care (DPC) through their benefits plans.

Nothing will transform healthcare more than employers like these, with such a large number of employees adopting this new model. If other companies don't get on board with a cheaper, better healthcare system, employers like EY will outcompete those companies for the best talent.

YOUR TICKET TO ATTRACT AND RETAIN TALENT

As a CEO, your employees are your business's greatest asset. They're what keeps it running—there literally would be no business without them. And the value of those employees is increased by their talent, motivation, work ethic, and values. If you've had a really excellent employee, you understand the value they bring to the company is irreplaceable, even if you could find someone else to fill their shoes.

What's more, the cost of replacing an employee is high. While the data varies greatly depending on industry and other factors, statistics show that it costs anywhere between 50-150% of their annual salary, on average, to replace an employee. That cost comes partially from hiring and training a replacement, but also from a loss in productivity not just in the absence of that person's role but also in the increased workload of other employees who have to pick up the slack. Those other employees may not be able to perform their own jobs at the top of their skill level as a result.

Every time an employee leaves, it causes a ripple effect throughout your business, affecting it in ways that may not be immediately apparent. It also tends to decrease morale, and losing one top-performing employee can sometimes lead to losing more.

According to the Bureau of Labor Statistics, in 2022, Americans had a median tenure of 4.3 years for men and 3.9 years for women, though these numbers are higher for older workers than for younger ones. Many employees change jobs every few years, often because it's the only way they can achieve an increase in compensation that keeps them at a competitive pay level. And benefits play an important role in that compensation package, especially for employees who are looking for more than just a salary increase.

The people in our teams matter deeply. In some industries, employee turnover matters less than in others—and you know your priorities best—but if you're purchasing healthcare to retain and attract high-value employees who will contribute to the profitability of your business, your healthcare offerings are an important part of their benefits incentive.

Not only does aspirational healthcare allow you to create a healthier workforce through relationship-based healthcare, but it also improves your retention by creating happier employees who trust you. As a result, they are likely to be more invested in their roles.

If your employer provided the best healthcare you'd ever had in your life, where you had a strong relationship with your doctor and a coach to help you reach your goals, and all of it cost you less than you paid with health insurance, would you be hesitant to leave? I know I certainly would, and my employees agree. They don't want to go back to the traditional healthcare system, and the healthcare they receive through me has created a relationship of trust knowing I have their best interests at heart.

When employees have relationships with people they trust and they access that relationship through you, they will stay with you.

Right now, the majority of healthcare offered to employees in the U.S. is transactional. But every business is built on relationships, and healthcare should be no different.

John Keller, the president of Redlist, described the benefits of implementing an aspirational model in his business as twofold: not only did it save them money, but it also created a cultural shift through an increased understanding among employees of what was going on within their healthcare as well as an increased energy in their work and personal lives.

The cultural impacts of an aspirational healthcare model likely aren't the first things many business leaders think of—we don't tend to associate healthcare with workplace culture, after all. But it absolutely has a significant effect on culture, and culture is one of the primary factors in employee attraction and retention.

So how did Redlist do it? As they implemented their aspirational model, they prioritized two goals and set up dashboards to let them monitor their progress on those two goals:

1. Create more awareness and power for employees to make decisions

2. Avoid increased costs to put more money back into employees' pockets

Employees benefited from becoming active consumers and having agency within their healthcare rather than depending on a disinterested third party like an insurance company to make decisions for them. And their workplace culture was further strengthened by implementing wellness coaching, helping individuals reach their goals and live healthier lives overall.

STRENGTHEN YOUR WORKPLACE CULTURE

Aspirational healthcare improves your competitive advantage in the employer marketplace by adding to your benefits package, but its power to change your workplace culture goes far beyond just a new healthcare benefit. I can say from experience that aspirational healthcare has certainly added to our culture at Orriant.

While a workplace culture is made up of all the individuals who are a part of it, those in leadership positions have the largest influence on the culture. Anyone who has ever worked for a bad boss can tell you how detrimental it is to the culture. Conversely, a great boss who cares about their people can foster a positive and motivating environment. The best leaders out there know how to invest in their teams and support them on a personal level to reach their dreams and goals. And that's what aspirational healthcare is all about.

By giving people support to control their healthcare costs while reaching their dreams, you create immense loyalty because they know the leadership cares about their personal well-being.

Just like supporting people to reach their aspirations helps them become healthier, it also affects other areas of their lives. Employees who are happy and healthy tend to be more positive and energetic and bring that energy to work with them, which has a significant effect on culture. Doing the right thing in healthcare is also the right thing for culture.

Supporting people to reach their aspirations is just as important in business as it is in healthcare. It is one of the most important things you can do to create culture. The book *It's Your Ship* by Captain Michael Abrashoff[9] tells a story about a Navy officer who was given responsibility for the worst-performing battleship in the Navy. He was the youngest admiral to be put in charge of a battleship and he put into practice continuous quality improvement strategies.

Because nobody stayed on the ship for more than three or four years, the officer met with each person individually and asked them what they wanted to do in the long term after their time on the ship was over. Once he understood their aspirations, he made sure they were assigned positions that would prepare them to be really good at what they wanted to do in the future. He wanted to give them the chance to develop their skills, so if they want to be a carpenter, a plumber, or a manager, they would have the ability to do that. He made sure that everybody on the ship was aligned to support each other in their dreams. As a result, his ship became the best-performing battleship in the Navy.

I highly recommend the book *The Dream Manager* by Matthew Kelly, a fictitious story about a CEO who was struggling with high employee turnover and hired a dream manager. The dream manager's job was to support employees in reaching their personal goals, dreams, and aspirations in life. The high turnover problem went away.[10]

I also recommend the book *The Go-Giver* for leadership.[11] If you want to succeed, always expect to give more than you receive. In the context of employment, the same thing applies—the more you give your employees, the more they will give back to you, and the more loyal they will become.

One strategy can accomplish many goals. By offering your employees a personal success coach, you improve employee health and productivity, drive down the long-term cost of healthcare, and create an amazingly loyal workforce.

Misunderstandings About Aspirational Healthcare

Employees would rather keep their familiar health insurance, so aspirational healthcare won't help me attract or retain employees.

Remember that choice is one of the foundational principles of aspirational healthcare—employees get to choose the design of their healthcare benefits. If they want traditional health insurance, let them have it! There are a number of ways you can offer that option while incentivizing them to choose other options, which we'll go into more detail about later. Your employees who take advantage of the new benefits you offer them will often be your best ambassadors for the new options and will encourage other employees to use them as well.

CHAPTER 7

A New Front Door to Healthcare

Hospital administrators, like I was once, acquire physician practices because they are the funnel source to bring patients into the healthcare system. When a physician orders a CAT scan, they order it through the hospital system they belong to. That way, the hospital can charge $3,000 for it even if across the street, the independent imaging center only charges $300.

To emphasize this point, I will tell you about an experience I had attending a healthcare leadership conference at Brigham Young University. One of the speakers was a gentleman from Providence, a healthcare system in the Northwest. He put a slide on the screen showing something that everyone in healthcare knows but rarely wants to admit—I couldn't believe that he was actually showing it as a part of his presentation. The slide showed three boxes: The first two boxes were titled "Patients of Our Employed Primary Care Providers" and "Employed Specialists," and both had two red dollar signs above them, representing that Providence loses money by owning both of these practices. There were arrows pointing from these boxes to the next, titled "More Desirable Referral Flow."

The third box on the right was titled "Providence Hospitals, ASCs (ambulatory surgical centers), Imaging Centers, Etc." Above that box were two large green dollar signs, representing that this is where Providence makes money.

Those of us in the healthcare industry all know this is how healthcare works, but I had never seen anyone brave enough to put it on a slide. I raised my hand and said that the largest employers in the country have figured this out and are now paying 100% for their employees to see independent primary care providers to avoid this funnel source.

His response shocked me. He said, "Nothing could be better for the American people!"

His next slide showed news releases demonstrating how primary care is being disrupted by large companies like Walmart, Amazon, Walgreens, and CVS. His whole message to the conference attendees was that traditional healthcare funnel sources are being disrupted, and that in the future healthcare is going to have to compete based on cost and quality instead of owning the funnel sources. I was very impressed with his message!

The motivational alignment that affects health outcomes and controls costs starts at the front door.

The beauty of advanced primary care is that it changes the provider's incentives. No longer is their incentive to provide services for a fee, therefore earning more money by increasing the number of services they do; instead, their incentive is to keep your employees healthy and keep your costs down. By doing so, you unshackle the primary care physician from the insurance industry that keeps them from being able to care for the patient in the best way possible.

I suggest that employees have a relationship with three individuals to fully benefit from the AH model:

- A navigator to help them navigate the system

- A primary care practitioner who gets to know them and coordinates all their care

- A health coach who partners with them to help them live life to its fullest

Advanced primary care is surprisingly simple to build into your healthcare plan, and the benefits are enormous. You simply create a defined contribution, which could be anywhere from $50-$150 a month per employee or per member, in order to offer your employees a different front door to the healthcare system. From there, let them choose which advanced primary care plan they'd like. If they want to purchase one that costs more, deduct it from their payroll, and if they choose one that costs less, let them keep the leftover money. If they would rather stick with their traditional insurance for primary care, let them, but don't give them the money. The point of spending that money per month is to give them a different experience with healthcare.

Choice is one of the primary principles of aspirational healthcare, and your role as an employer is simply to give them the opportunity to enter the healthcare system a different way.

MAKE ADVANCED PRIMARY CARE EASY

There are already a number of advanced primary care (APC) networks available to choose from, and you may be surprised at how affordable they are.

There are organizations that bring networks of subscription-based advanced primary care providers together to make it easy for employers to offer this service to their employees. Apaly, Nexus Health Connect, and Hint are some of these types of organizations.

A good example of one of these networks of APC providers is Nice Healthcare, which we partner with frequently. They have an excellent and growing subscription-based primary care solution that is available in many metropolitan areas across the country. It's amazing what you get for a fraction of the cost.

First, and most importantly, you get a relationship with a primary care provider. They get to know you and you get to know them. At any time, you can schedule a chat, a visit, or a video call. Getting in touch is easy, and much of what you need can be handled over the phone. That primary care provider can call in a prescription for you, which you can pick up or have sent to your home, and over 500 medications are included in the cost of the primary care (to learn more about coverage for medications, see chapter 9).

When you need to be seen in person for any reason, such as for blood work, an X-ray, or your annual physical, that primary provider comes to your home or your office.

In addition to primary care, Nice Healthcare also includes mental health services and physical therapy.

Nice Healthcare isn't the only advanced primary care option available, but it serves as an excellent example of how employers can offer a better front door to healthcare. It's healthcare built around the person.

ADVANCED PRIMARY CARE IS LIKE A DOCTOR IN YOUR POCKET

One experience I had after breaking my ankle really demonstrated to me how different advanced primary care is from traditional primary care.

At the time, I'd been given the opportunity to be the opening keynote speaker at a large employer healthcare conference in Washington, D.C.—it was a huge opportunity for me. However, a week before the conference, I had an accident.

I was picking apples in my backyard and saw an apple up high in the middle of the tree that I couldn't reach. I moved the ladder toward it and climbed up, but as I did, the branches pushed the ladder over, and I fell. I knew my ankle was badly hurt, so I wobbled into the house. I had two options: I could go to urgent care, or I could schedule a chat session with my primary care provider and ask them to send an X-ray machine to my home. So that's what I did, and it didn't cost me a penny to have the X-ray machine come out the next morning. Sure enough, I had a broken ankle.

Once I knew it was broken, I had to schedule an appointment with an orthopedic surgeon. The ankle would likely need surgery. Of course, I was worried about how I would get across the country to do the presentation—I certainly didn't want to have to cancel. I asked my provider, "Are they going to let me on the plane?"

Because my primary care provider knew I was anxious about making it to my presentation, she came with me virtually to meet with the surgeon and make sure the surgeon knew how important it was to me to be able to get to my conference. The doctor said, "As long as it's not causing you a tremendous amount of pain and you're willing to fly, you can go do your presentation at the conference. The bone has broken off and you can't make it any worse than it is. As soon as you get back, we'll do the needed surgery."

In the end, I was able to get up on stage and it didn't even look like I had a broken ankle. Having a relationship with a primary care provider who knew my needs and was protecting my greater well-being made me feel taken care of. It was very convenient, and I received a high level of care.

I'm not the only one who has had a great experience with advanced primary care. One of my team members, Bob, broke his thumb. Here's how he tells the story:

I love to get up high and enjoy the beautiful Rocky Mountain vistas. And that is exactly what I was enjoying early one morning. I was not as high up in the mountain trails as I normally love to go. I was out for a quick early morning street ride, when out of the blue, I ran smack directly into a concrete barrier right in the middle of a very long parking lot. And I was not going slow.

The bike made it over the barrier, but not without first imposing an amazing amount of damage to both of my hands because my thumbs were wrapped around the handlebar and therefore bore the brunt of the impact. Once the front wheel cleared the barrier, it was the rear wheel's turn to deliver its medicine. Without as significant of a shock absorption mechanism as the front wheel, I was trajected upward and forward over the handlebar. I landed forcefully on my head and shoulder. The bike and I came to a final rest no less than 20 feet from the point of impact. I have repeated visions of the pavement defying gravity and momentum as it rose from its normal stationary horizontal position and came with unimaginable speed and force directly toward my face. Fortunately, I somehow managed to turn my head in time to preserve my nose. My heavy-duty ski helmet (yes, it was cold, so I grabbed this amazingly comfortable and warm industrial-strength ski helmet rather than my normal bike helmet, which would not have fared as well) protected my intellect and surrounding infrastructure.

Somehow, I managed to ride my bike down the hill all the way home while sporting injuries on my shoulder, thumbs, wrists, hands, knees, and ankle.

Most of my injuries were superficial. My two thumbs, however, were a longer-term project. One thumb was fractured, and the other hand had a bruised ligament governing the thumb. Basically, I could not use either thumb.

As soon as I arrived home from my accident, I scheduled a virtual meeting with my doctor. I was able to meet my doctor almost immediately. I uploaded photos of my injuries. My doctor advised how to care for each of my wounds. Then she arranged for an X-ray technician to bring a portable X-ray machine to my home. Without leaving my home, I was able to have a doctor's appointment, treat my wounds, have an X-ray, and receive the radiologist report—all on the same day as my accident.

There was no ER visit. No waiting in a doctor's office. No deductible. No copay. No out of pocket. No expense. That's because I have a subscription to healthcare that covers my primary and preventive healthcare through Nice Healthcare. It covers a lot of things actually, including my physical therapy. It also includes a formulary of over 550 common prescription medications that are 100% covered with no deductible, no copay—no out-of-pocket expense. And it includes in-home labs.

A subscription to this innovative new approach to healthcare is much less expensive than purchasing healthcare through traditional healthcare plans. And the convenience is amazing.

Misunderstandings About Aspirational Healthcare

It's too difficult to change.

Do you want to take on the problem of solving the cost of healthcare, or do you want to just keep thinking about it as a required expenditure that goes up every year?

Making a change starts with simply defining your objectives. With the help of a company like mine, Orriant, you can set up a process to measure your objectives and start making the healthcare system accountable in order to cut your costs. It's not difficult to do; you just need to overcome a little bit of inertia to get started.

Doctors won't accept subscriptions instead of insurance.

If employers are willing to build the demand, I have yet to meet a primary care physician who wanted to stay in the old system. Physicians can make more money on a subscription-based model, have more time to spend with their patients, and have their incentives aligned with their purpose. Most physicians hate the current system—they feel it's a rat race.

Employers who adopt an aspirational healthcare model don't have a problem with finding providers—what we have is a problem with demand because people don't know this system exists. CEOs are the best people to drive that demand as the primary purchasers of healthcare benefit programs.

There is already a shortage of primary care providers.
Some would say that we already have a shortage of primary care providers, and if providers have smaller patient panels, the shortage will only get larger. However, this perspective fails to account for the reason there is a shortage: providers dislike the conditions of their jobs and the current system, which has driven many to leave primary care.

Give providers fewer patients and the time to create trusting relationships with their patients, and they will want to go into primary care. Primary care providers can also make more money under this model of care, making it a more attractive and sustainable career option than primary care under the current system. Nurse practitioners and physician assistants make very effective primary care providers and will fill a large part of the growing demand for subscription-based primary care providers.

CHAPTER 8

Leverage the Power of Cash

Of course, healthcare doesn't stop at primary care. While an advanced primary care plan covers many of a family's healthcare needs, specialists and catastrophic care must also be accounted for. How you go about offering these as an employer may differ, based on the size of your organization and whether you self-fund your plan or offer a defined contribution for employees to purchase their own healthcare benefits.

A self-funded plan means that you as an employer pay for healthcare services rather than purchasing insurance that's responsible for paying claims. If you purchase insurance, you're already paying for the cost of those healthcare services along with the profit the insurance company makes off the interaction, so self-funding allows you to cut out those profits by paying for services yourself.

Self-funded healthcare plans have been used by larger employers for quite some time. Simply purchasing an insurance plan for your employees will never save you money, because there's no incentive for an insurance company to bring your costs down. In fact, buying insurance locks you into major cost increases every year. In order to keep costs manageable, many employers self-fund their healthcare plans, paying claims directly in order to save on markups the insurance company would charge to pay those claims for you. Generally, self-funded plans are used by companies with 50 employees or more, though in some states, you need to have 100 or more.

The way self-funded plans typically work is through a third-party administrator. You have a benefits advisor consultant help you work with that third-party administrator who takes care of paying the claims using your money. As the employer, you take on the risk of claims up to a certain point—a corridor of risk that you determine, whether that's $75,000 or $150,000. If a claim goes over that amount, you cover it with a reinsurance policy—once you pay the initial determined amount, the reinsurance will cover everything beyond that point. This eliminates taking on the risk of particularly large claims and allows you as an employer to determine how much risk you're willing to take on for the savings you receive through self-funding.

Be careful to sign a reinsurance policy that doesn't include language allowing the carrier to renege on paying high claims. Also avoid language that allows for laser claims, which are catastrophic claimants on the plan where the carrier may wish to require a separate, individual-specific high deductible that applies to a single identified person.

Many self-funded employers also use captives before reinsurance, which are a group of other employers who together create a reinsurance-type pool with each other. Any unused money in the pool goes back to the employers after the end of the year. With a reinsurance policy, any money you put into it is gone for good. But with a captive between your reinsurance and your pool of risk, you can cover many costs without using reinsurance and anything you put in that wasn't used comes back to you.

When you step back and think about how insurance companies make money, self-funding makes a lot of sense. The insurance company has to charge an amount that's larger than what they'll actually pay out in claims in order to make a profit, and as the purchaser of insurance, you'll never get that money back. If you self-fund your plan, you can break up the amount you would spend on health insurance between what you spend on claims, the cost of processing those claims, and the cost of reinsurance. Whatever is left over you get to keep.

For a monthly fee, the third-party administrator also gives your employees access to a network of providers, which gives you access to contracted rates with various doctors and hospitals. Most employers will encourage their employees to go to providers within this network in order to pay less money.

However, self-funded plans can now use a different strategy to lower costs even more while also improving the quality of care they provide. New hospital transparency laws have created an environment that allows this new strategy to be even more effective by leveraging the power of cash.

MAKING THE MOST OF PRICING TRANSPARENCY

You can often save more money on healthcare using a cash pay discount than through your network contracts. And now you can know the cash price and quality of a procedure ahead of time and even use it to help you choose where to get treatment.

It all starts with the new transparency rules—the Hospital Price Transparency Rule and the Transparency in Coverage Rule—which took effect in 2021.[12] These rules, which were hard fought for, were designed to give consumers visibility into all negotiated rates (which vary by 10 times within the same hospital and by 31 times across hospitals) as well as the discounted cash prices.

Recently, an industry-favorable bill was introduced in the House of Representatives that would allow estimated prices in lieu of real prices for hospitals' cash prices. This proposed provision was an anti-competitive maneuver by the insurance industry to make the cash price seem higher than insured rates. The nonprofit Patient Rights Advocate organization (PatientRightsAdvocate.org) put out a campaign to fight the rollback, including a commercial showing how impractical it is to use estimated costs—imagine if everything you purchased was only a cost estimate and you were given a surprise bill in the mail later that you were on the hook for! What would it be like to buy a cup of coffee and not know if it would cost $3 or $30 until your bill arrived? That's similar to how estimated pricing in healthcare would work.

A stronger bipartisan bill, the Healthcare PRICE Transparency Act 2.0, introduced in the Senate by Senators Bernie Sanders and Mike Braun, would codify the hospital and insurer price transparency rules for all actual prices, and would empower employer and union health plans to access a daily feed of their claims, billing, and payment data, so they can be in control, get rid of administrative waste, and eliminate fraud, errors, and overcharges. This bill would give the true purchasers—consumers, unions, and employers—the ability to benefit from competition and have remedy and recourse if they're overcharged. Healthcare price transparency from hospitals and insurers is still the rule of law, and it has changed the way many organizations are approaching healthcare.

The new law requires hospitals to publicly disclose somewhere on their websites the costs for different procedures. I recently downloaded this information—a document called a "machine-readable pricing file"—for one of the largest hospitals in Utah and found that, out of all the contracts the hospital signed, the average discount they gave to those they contracted with was 30%. But for people who paid cash outside of a network contract, the discount was 75%.

What does that mean in practice? If you had a liver transplant at that hospital, it would cost $325,795 as their base price, for example. If you paid for it through a network contract, the average price would be $226,960. However, if you said, "Put it on my credit card," the cash price would be $81,449.

You might think this is an anomaly—after all, it's just one example in Utah. But it's actually a pattern in hospitals across the U.S. For one of the largest hospitals in Washington, D.C., the average discount with an insurance contract is 39%, and the average cash discount is 60%.

Because hospitals are required to share their chargemaster documents publicly, there are now websites and businesses that have gathered that pricing information from all the hospitals in the country and make it available to you for free. You can look up any procedure at any hospital, and you'll find not only the base price, but the cash price and the price for every contract. The Patient Rights Advocate organization (PatientRightsAdvocate.org) is a good resource to use in researching prices, through the Hospital Price Files Finder (HospitalPricingFiles.org).

It's shockingly common to find enormous differences in contracted prices for the same procedures. You might find one procedure costs $4,000 under one contract and $24,000 under another.

What does this mean for the employer who wishes to spend less on healthcare? It wouldn't be fair for you to simply give your employees these tools and ask them to shop around to find the best price for their healthcare procedures—most people would find that overwhelming and difficult. However, you can offer your employees a navigator who can do all the hard work, and then you use a self-funded plan to pay the cash price for whatever your employees need. Because you will save so much money, this model allows you to completely waive all copays, deductibles, co-insurance, and out-of-pocket maximums—which is an excellent incentive to your employees to use this self-funded, cash-pay option.

Organizations that have been using this system to purchase healthcare for their employees are sometimes paying less than 50% of what they otherwise would have paid by simply paying directly and up front.

A complete transformation of healthcare is possible by simply spending your money differently.

Even if they don't put a cash pay price online, most hospitals will give you a discount if you pay cash up front. Why? Having been a hospital controller, CFO, and administrator, I know that an unimaginable amount of money goes into collecting money from insurance companies. I ran a whole army of people getting pre-authorizations, making sure we were accredited so that we could have a contract with the insurance company, making sure the insurance company paid us within a reasonable amount of time, coding everything to maximize reimbursement, and fighting with the insurance company when they denied claims. This whole army worked to get as much money out of the insurance company as possible for every procedure. If you pay with cash up front, of course the hospital will give you a discount, because they bypass all that work on the back end.

There are two primary ways you can use this pricing transparency data to save money on secondary or catastrophic healthcare: through a cash-pay plan like I just mentioned, or through reference-based pricing.

Cash Pay

First, ensure that your employees have access to subscription-based advanced primary care. For secondary care—say they need to see a specialist—set up your self-funded plan with reinsurance to limit your risk. This way, all of your employees are covered under your insurance plan so both of you will have peace of mind. However, ask them to put their insurance card away somewhere safe and never use it—instead, give them a company debit card with a limit on it, which they can use to pay cash for their healthcare. As long as they use this card, they won't have to pay copays or co-insurance—their healthcare will be completely covered by you and you will both get to pay a lot less for healthcare.

Then, when they need to see a doctor, instruct them to simply walk into the doctor's office and say, "I'll be paying cash," and use the card you've given them. People have the legal right not to tell their provider that they have insurance if they are paying cash at the time of service. You don't want to disclose that you have insurance because then the doctor will want to receive their contracted insurance rate, which is often more than the cash pay rate.

Now, this card won't have enough money to pay for a $100,000 surgery, but if a major procedure is needed, the employee contacts your third-party administrator who will help them navigate to the best outcome provider and negotiate with the hospital to ensure you're paying the best price. The third-party administrator then puts the needed money on the card to pay upfront for the procedure. This way, you can still pay cash without putting a large chunk of money on everyone's cards.

There are companies who facilitate a cash-pay strategy for your self-funded plan. They make it easy for you to leverage the power of cash payments for medical care. One of those companies is Asserta Health.

Reference-Based Pricing

Reference-based pricing is another strategy that many employers have used to save a lot of money, but it comes with some headaches.

Reference-based pricing (RBP) is a strategy where the employer pays a reasonable amount for a medical procedure based on what Medicare pays that hospital for that procedure rather than paying the provider's billed amount, which is often many times higher than the provider accepts from the government. Providers are asked to accept the RBP payment as payment in full or provide justification as to why their fees exceed reasonable and customary charges.

Like cash-pay, you set up a self-funded plan without network contracts. Your third-party administrator manages the plan, and your employees go wherever they want for healthcare. Then the third-party administrator looks up the Medicare rate for the employee's procedure because that information is publicly available. They'll usually pay the hospital 150-200% of

Medicare and send the hospital a check for that amount. If the hospital bills the patient $8,000, and the Medicare price is $2,000, the TPA might pay $4,000, which would be 200% of the Medicare price.

I'm not a fan of this model for this reason: When the hospital sees that you're not going to pay them the extra $4,000, they often go after the employee for the money. Obviously, this creates a stressful situation for that employee. Then the third-party administrator will bring their attorneys in and argue that the cost isn't reasonable, and it has the potential to wind up in court.

This strategy can be a good way to save a lot of money, but it can cause a lot of pain for your employees. While in many cases the hospital will accept the RBP payment, some will bill the patient for the balance. If you're going to use reference-based pricing, please don't put your employees in the middle—just settle with the hospital directly and let your employees know that they won't be on the hook for a balance if the hospital will not settle.

As you can probably imagine, the American Hospital Association (AHA) is not a fan of RBP plans. If you are interested in learning why the AHA believes RBP pricing is bad, access and read their position paper.[13]

There are many referenced-based pricing companies on the market that can help you leverage this strategy in your plan. They can help save your company a lot of money—just don't put your employees at risk for the bills they may receive from the hospital.

Both of these options are far better than paying for access to a network. When you pay for a network, you're primarily offering your employees hospital-owned providers, which ends up feeding the dragon of the healthcare industry.

CUSTOMIZE YOUR PLAN DESIGN

There are many ways to customize your aspirational healthcare design for your organization and the needs of your employees. We've been discussing the benefits of self-funding, but this approach won't work for smaller employers, and there are other factors that may influence the way you design your plan.

There is no single right way to do aspirational healthcare, and there are a number of possible plan designs that work very well. For the sake of this book, I will outline two primary plan designs, which I see as the optimal approaches for large employers and small employers.

However, aspirational healthcare isn't limited to just these plan designs. Think of them as a base plan from which you can make adjustments based on the needs of your company and your employees. An important aspect of an aspirational healthcare strategy is continually improving the strategy (that is, continuous quality improvement, CQI) to meet your goals.

The customizability of aspirational healthcare is one of the reasons it's so important to work with a benefits advisor who is aligned with your interests to ensure you choose the options that will help you reach your goals for purchasing healthcare. Insist that your benefits advisor is a certified aspirational healthcare advisor (CAA).

CHAPTER 9

The Aspirational Strategy for Medium and Large Employers

For companies that are large enough, the best way to save on health-care costs while providing the best care is to create a self-funded plan using a navigator to direct employees to the best outcome providers at the best price. In addition to the self-funded plan, this healthcare design option should include subscription-based advanced primary care and health coaching services.

Many companies across the country have saved significant amounts of money by creating an innovative self-funded plan using the following strategies, tools, and vendors:

1. **Innovative Third-Party Administrators (TPA)**

   The major insurance carriers like Cigna, Aetna, and United Healthcare offer TPA services. In fact, providing TPA services to self-funded employers is one of the biggest parts of their business. I highly recommend that you steer away from their administrative services only (ASO) contracts. You won't find significant savings through an ASO contract with a large carrier. They will promote how easy it is to set up your self-funded plan through them, but you are applying the same broken system that they use for their fully insured clients. And in many cases, you are getting far less control over the way your plan operates.

It's best to work with innovative TPAs who are willing to help you set up innovative plans to increase employee satisfaction and save money. The biggest challenge employers face using these independent TPAs is the pressure from their employees to see those big industry names like Cigna, Aetna, and United Healthcare on their insurance cards. This hurdle may require some education on your part to help your employees understand how healthcare works and that you want something better for them.

2. Reinsurance Carriers

Unless you are an employer with tens of thousands of members on your health plan and are prepared to take the financial risk for all healthcare costs, you should have a reinsurance policy in place to cover large spike claims and aggregate claims beyond your willingness to risk. Finding a reinsurance carrier who will give you credit for all of the innovative strategies you want to put in place to save money may be your most difficult task. Work with a good benefit consultant who can guide you through this process.

3. Healthcare Captives

Many employers have leveraged the benefits of joining a healthcare captive. This is where a group of employers create a risk pool that sits under your reinsurance policy and above your company's risk capacity for your self-funded plan. The big advantage of a healthcare captive is that the run-off risk is fairly short, much shorter than captives in many other industries. That means if providers don't submit bills for their services in a timely manner, they lose the right to bill. This means that any excess from the captive pool can return to the captive members within the next year.

4. Subscription-Based Advanced Primary Care Networks

If all your employees are in one general area, you can find a local APC to contract with who will likely be willing to visit your members at your workplace if you will provide them with a meeting place. In most cases, it can just be an open office where they can set up their special equipment. If your employees are spread out geographically, you will want to engage with a network of APCs across the country. (Another term used in the industry for APC is direct primary care (DPC).)

5. Pharmacy Benefit Management (PBM)

Every plan will need to manage the cost of prescriptions, which is not done through the TPA (third-party administrator) but rather through a PBM. In setting up your own self-funded plan, you will need a PBM as discussed in chapter 3. You definitely want to work with a *transparent* PBM, but be aware that they are all beginning to leverage that word and calling themselves transparent PBMs. As described earlier, the only way to get around the games they play is to insist that your PBM contract spell out the end-user cost of every drug on your formulary. Then use market forces to drive down that price on a continual basis.

6. Specialty Pharmacy Manager

Almost half of your pharmacy costs will be spent on a very tiny number of your members. Specialty drugs can cost as much as $2 million a year for one prescription. Some of them are very effective drugs—especially the biological drugs—but the costs are high, so it is important to contract with a vendor who specializes in managing the costs of these specialty drugs.

7. Healthcare Cost and Quality Navigation

Now that hospitals and insurance companies are required by law to post their prices online, there are vendors who have access to all that data and will support your members by navigating them to the providers who get the best outcomes at the best price.

8. Surgery Networks

The costs of surgeries are often one of the biggest expenses of a health plan. The costs associated with surgeries can vary immensely, and many independent surgical centers across the country provide higher quality care and are willing to bundle their surgical procedures and guarantee the price up front. The Surgical Center of Oklahoma City is a great example of this and they have pioneered a movement that has spread across the country. Contracting with a network of surgical providers who offer bundled prices is a needed part of your self-funded plan. You can create significant benefit design incentives for your members to use these options by removing any copay or deductibles, if they go to one of these providers.

9. Organ Transplant Assistance

One member of your plan needing an organ transplant can easily cost your plan hundreds of thousands of dollars. In the case of a liver transplant, the cost of dialysis alone can quickly eat up your funds. There are vendors who assist with both managing dialysis costs and coordinating the process of getting a transplant surgery scheduled for your member to receive a new liver and go off of dialysis.

10. Diabetes Care

Diabetes is often best managed by a good concierge primary care provider, backed up by a good endocrinologist. Encouraging the use of subscription-based advanced primary care is your best solution for managing the costs of diabetes.

11. Musculoskeletal Care

About half of all Americans suffer from some kind of chronic pain. There are vendors who specialize in back, neck, and joint pain, which compose the second most common reason to visit a doctor. However, these ailments are commonly mistreated, resulting in unnecessary surgeries and the overuse of painkillers. My own experience has been remarkable. After dealing with numbness in my arms and hands at night when I sleep on my side and trying physical therapy recommended by my primary care provider, I felt no relief until I had one visit with a musculoskeletal specialist. By doing a few simple recommended stretches, the numbness was almost gone in one day.

12. Infertility Vendors

There are vendors who provide expert care to those seeking to begin a family and who are struggling with infertility. These vendors reduce the incidence of high-risk NICU and multiples (twins and triplets) and help people get pregnant at lower cost, quickly, and with better outcomes.

13. Psychiatry Network Vendors

One of the most prevalent provider shortages across the country is in the area of psychiatry. With or without offering your members a network of providers that includes psychiatrists, your members will struggle to get in and see someone, especially a child psychiatrist. These network vendors provide a higher level of access to these providers, who are becoming more and more needed all the time.

14. Cancer Centers of Excellence

Cancer is one of the most complex and quickly changing diseases in the world. It's also one of the most lethal illnesses many people will ever face. There are cancer programs that employers can partner up with that provide the patient an expert second opinion from a global cancer center of excellence near the patient.

15. Readmission Prevention Vendors

Unnecessary readmissions to hospitals can cost a lot of money and can often be prevented. These vendors follow up with each patient and their caregivers immediately following discharge and make sure that the discharge plan is being followed. This simple follow-up over the first few days after discharge can have a significant impact on preventing readmissions.

16. Telemedicine and Teletherapy

Although the best solution to provide telemedicine to your members is through subscription-based advanced primary care, some of your members will choose to stay with their healthcare system-owned provider. By offering them telemedicine and teletherapy services, many of their immediate healthcare needs can be met virtually. It can also bring your costs down significantly for these services.

17. Hazardous Prescription Protection Vendors

Personalized support from a clinical pharmacist can make sure medications are working their best and reduce side effects for your members. Through these vendors, pharmacists review the patients and the medications being taken to find dangerous drug mixes or gaps, and they engage directly with the physicians caring for those members to resolve hazardous drug regimens.

18. Fraud and Abuse

There are vendors who can catch fraud and abuse in the claims you receive. Vendors analyze your claims to find carefully concealed fraud and stop it.

19. Coaching Vendors

My company Orriant is a coaching vendor and was one of the first in the country. We partner with many of the subscription-based advanced primary care providers to integrate coaching into the primary care clinical team, dramatically improving outcomes.

20. Concierge Customer Service

Your TPA vendor will offer you a standard level of customer service. However, if you really want your employees to be taken care of with white gloves, engage the services of a vendor who moves customer service to a whole new level. Because this is the front door to many of your employees' experiences with the healthcare system, it can make a huge difference when they have 24/7 access and are treated with the greatest care and respect each time. Often concierge vendors will provide more than just customer service to answer billing questions and questions about network availability. By also offering care coordination, navigation, pre-authorization, utilization review/management, and case management, these vendors can provide a concierge level of service for your members through every interaction with the health plan.

21. Consumer Engagement Tool Vendors

Your employees are looking for consumer tools that make accessing healthcare services simple. Imagine what your employees' healthcare experiences would be like with an AI-powered employee benefits app. In today's world of technology, your employees are looking for real-time, personalized answers on benefits coverage, treatment options, and preventive care tips.

Finding and signing contracts with all these different vendors can be a lot of work. Also, many of them charge on a per-employee per-month (PEPM) basis. They get paid whether their service is used or not. This can erode a lot of your savings and you wind up not saving much at all.

The good news is that two very influential industry leaders have come together to disrupt the American healthcare system. These two industry leaders are Lee Lewis, chief strategy officer (CSO) and general manager of medical solutions for the Health Transformation Alliance, and Heidi Cottle, senior vice president of cost containment strategies at NFP, an Aon company. In a collaborative effort, they have created a solution that brings all this together for employers across the U.S. This solution is open-source and can be white labeled. It gives any employer large enough to be self-funded access to all these solutions together under one elegant plan design.

We at Orriant have white labeled this self-funded option and call it the Super Plan. This plan does all the work for you, and you get all the bells and whistles of the very best self-funded plan design with only a single contract, rather than having to set up multiple contracts with all the various vendors.

WHAT IS THE SUPER PLAN?

The Super Plan is a customizable self-funded plan that includes all 21 tools and strategies described above. Additionally, it was built to make it easy to add on additional point solutions as needed.

The best part is that through the Super Plan, you don't pay any of those vendors and point solutions by a PEPM (monthly fee per employee) except for the third-party administrator. Every vendor has agreed to provide their services on a per-use basis, which gets billed as a claim through the TPA. This is the most transformable solution this country has ever seen in the healthcare industry.

When your employees use any of the point solutions, it will save you a lot of money and they avoid having to pay any copays or deductibles, which creates an amazing incentive for your employees to access these services. Imagine what your health plan dashboard would look like with all of these services offered.

Essentially, the Super Plan covers almost everything you need to set up your self-funded aspirational healthcare plan, with two exceptions: it doesn't include an incentive for health coaching or an EBHRA health savings account for your employees, though we recommend that employers of all sizes still create both those things (more on both of these tools in chapter 10).

Using the Super Plan, employees have the option to enter the healthcare system through their advanced primary care provider, their coach, or any of the other services listed above, which you can think of as tier-one providers. For these services, the employee never has to pay copays or deductibles. (The only exception to this is if you offer a health savings account (HSA) along with an HSA-qualified high-deductible plan option to your employees. In this case, the government requires that the employee pay a fair market value for all healthcare services until they reach their deductible. This is necessary to prevent the employee who has an HSA from losing the tax advantages that go along with the HSA. However, a bill called the Primary Care Enhancement Act could change that.)

Then, when they need to access secondary care, the plan takes advantage of navigation with access to cost and quality transparency data as well as cash pay strategies to get the best care possible at the best rates possible. Our customer experience and navigation service, called White Glove Healthcare, directs employees to the best outcome providers at the best prices and leverages a variety of strategies to save you, the employer, a ton of money. The money you save allows you to reduce or eliminate any copays or co-insurance so your employees pay little or nothing for their secondary care as well.

Healthcare Transparency Resources Available to the Public

Sage Transparency – Employers' Forum of Indiana has created Sage Transparency™, a free, publicly accessible hospital price and quality dashboard. It is a browser-based dashboard that helps inform employers, policymakers, and others on the real prices that employers pay for hospital services across the country. Users can see prices from 2020 to 2022 for more than 4,000 hospitals and 2,000 ambulatory surgery centers (ASCs) nationwide along with brand-new drug price data for physician-administered medications. https://Dashboard.SageTransparency.org

Hospital Safety Grade – The Leapfrog Group has created a site that grades hospitals on various safety measures. For more than two decades, the Leapfrog Group has contributed to making the healthcare system better, improving the choices patients can make and preventing needless deaths. https://www.HospitalSafetyGrade.org

Turquoise Health – Turquoise Health has created a site that makes hospital prices and quality transparent for the public to see.
https://Turquoise.Health

Patient Rights Advocate Organization – This nonprofit organization fights for systemwide healthcare price transparency. They seek to empower patients and consumers with actual, upfront prices, greatly reducing healthcare costs through a functional, competitive market. They have gathered all the hospital pricing data and made it easy to read by the public. https://www.PatientRightsAdvocate.org

WHAT IS WHITE GLOVE HEALTHCARE?

White Glove Healthcare, provided by Orriant, serves as a one-of-a-kind concierge service for every aspect of healthcare, including concierge customer service, navigation, and coaching. With White Glove, all employees have to do is make one call, and they'll receive personalized service that helps them find the healthcare they need, answers their questions, and takes care of billing. They don't even have to call—they can chat, text, or send an email, and we're available 24/7 through https://Whiteglove.Healthcare to assist them.

White Glove allows you to ensure your employees take advantage of all the tier-one benefits of your Super Plan, which include subscription-based primary care providers you can contact day or night for a virtual call. In some cases, they will come to your home to make healthcare truly work for you.

White Glove coordinates with the advanced primary care providers and helps people access everything beyond primary care. We have access to one of the biggest databases of information on costs, appropriateness, and quality outcomes in the country, which allows us to connect employees with providers who have the highest ratings. As long as they go to the highest-rated providers, they can avoid paying copays or deductibles.

Of course, employees retain their choice. If they'd rather see a doctor who is not on our list—maybe their brother is a surgeon—they can do so, but they'll have to pay copays and deductibles for it.

Through White Glove Healthcare, Orriant offers your company a concierge service to a self-funded plan that we will help you set up. If your business is large enough to support a self-funded plan, this is the best option to save money and provide your employees with the highest quality healthcare available.

Orriant partners with a company through which you can find a subscription-based primary care provider in your area, learn details about them, and create an appointment. Let's say you're looking for a primary care doctor; you can do that by entering your location in their search function. It'll show you providers in your area, such as Nice Healthcare. You can sign up for care with a provider on their site and they send your information directly to the provider you selected. This company will handle the billing every month, and you now have subscription-based primary care in your pocket, and you don't have to worry about copays, deductibles, or payments. You just have a wonderful primary care experience.

White Glove also has access to the biggest database of providers across the country, including primary care doctors, specialists, surgical centers, imaging centers, and more. This database tracks their prices and the costs for services from all of these providers as well as data on appropriateness of treatments.

This database can search in any area of the country for any specialty, and it shows a rating for every provider that combines cost and quality information. It includes quality scores on a variety of metrics and information about which insurance networks the provider is contracted with. If an employer has a major insurance provider as part of their plan, through this database, we can help members find specialists who are in their networks.

This specialized database allows White Glove to locate healthcare providers with the best outcomes for the best prices. Their contract prices are already in place, so if we steer you toward that provider, you never have to pay any copays or deductibles and White Glove takes care of all required pre-authorizations.

White Glove is also able to leverage cash prices. For example, the most expensive procedure at one hospital is a liver transplant.

You can look up their fee schedule and see that the retail rate is $325,795, and the average rate for all of their contracts is $226,960 But it also shows a cash price: $81,449. So, if the best provider isn't in network, we can still access them through a contracted cash price.

White Glove is like your personal advocate—it's the one person you can call who will give you all the answers for whatever you happen to be going through to help you coordinate and navigate your care. If you just received a major diagnosis and don't know what the next steps are or how to explore your options, White Glove can walk you through it. For someone who was just told they have cancer or another major disease, navigating the next steps can be overwhelming, and White Glove is there to hold the patient's hand through the process.

Services Offered Through White Glove

- Coaching
- Inbound customer service
- Care coordination
- Care navigation when secondary care is needed
- Precertification
- Case management

STRATEGIES TO KEEP PRESCRIPTION COSTS LOW

One question you might have is about how employees pay for their prescriptions under the aspirational healthcare model. While this depends on the plan design you offer, there are a number of ways that you can minimize costs to your business and your employees.

If you have a self-funded healthcare plan, you need to understand how pharmacy benefit managers (PBMs) work.

PBMs are middlemen between drug manufacturers and patients. They often determine the costs the patients (and employers) pay for prescription drugs.

PBMs are responsible for many of the high prices on prescriptions that patients have to pay today. Why is that? There are just three large PBMs that represent the vast majority of the industry, and as such those large PBMs have a massive level of control over the price of drugs, as described in chapter 3.

PBMs are notorious for using formulas in their contracts to calculate price. The only real way to manage your pharmacy expenses and avoid these pricing games is by customizing your PBM contract. The contract should list out the *end-user cost* for every drug in your formulary. PBMs won't like it, and it represents some work in updating that contract regularly, but it is the only way to eliminate the formula games the PBMs play.

Additionally, you should look for a PBM that's transparent in how they make money. Not all PBMs are the same, and it's worth taking your time to research them before choosing one to contract with. Generally, if you avoid the big three and use alternative PBMs, you'll save money.

Why not just bypass PBMs altogether?

PBMs do offer one big advantage:
they help to eliminate dangerous drug interactions for
patients who need multiple prescriptions.

If all a patient's prescriptions are going through the PBM's technology platform, drugs that shouldn't be used at the same time can be caught and avoided.

However, you can also help your employees save money on prescriptions in other ways. Not all patients need to run their prescriptions through PBM services. For employees who are not taking multiple drugs at the same time, pharmacy discount programs offer some tremendous savings. For example, many people have a Costco membership but don't know that they have access to an amazing pharmacy discount program through Costco.

You can teach your employees who have Costco memberships to always fill their prescriptions at Costco. When they go to pay for their prescription, they can ask the Costco pharmacy staff to run the charges through both their insurance plan and their Costco membership discount program. Often when I do this, the price through the Costco discount program is substantially less than my copay through insurance.

By approaching prescriptions this way, you pay for the cost of the drug, which is often cheaper than the copay through insurance.

The Costco membership discount program isn't the only pharmacy discount program. Mark Cuban's Cost Plus Drugs is a discount program that will give you a better price on hundreds of drugs. Walmart also has a pharmacy program with a large number of drugs that are no more than $4. However, keep in mind that in many cases, the $4 is more than the actual cost of the drug if you run it through a discount program. There are a whole host of pharmacy discount programs that allow you to download a membership card online, such as GoodRx, SingleCare, and Wellex, and often the prices will be cheaper through these programs than the copay for the drug would be if you run it through the insurance plan.

All of these tools are available to lower the cost of prescriptions for your employees. If you're self-funded and working with a transparent PBM, it's still worthwhile to educate your employees about all of these discount options. Teach them to run their prescriptions through these discount options first to see if it'll be cheaper, and if not, then they can use their insurance card. The exception to this is if your members are on multiple drugs at the same time.

BREAKDOWN OF AN AH PLAN FOR MEDIUM TO LARGE EMPLOYERS

Let's review all of the components of the AH plan and how they work together to create a complete healthcare solution for medium size to large employers.

Setting up aspirational healthcare doesn't have to be difficult. In fact, it can all be done through a single contract with a variety of organizations such as Orriant, which use neutral, open-source database services to access cost savings and higher quality healthcare. Or you can build it yourself with the help of an experienced broker who is aligned with your business objectives.

1. For companies large enough to support a self-funded plan, all of your healthcare savings flow to your company's bottom line. By cutting out the middleman of the insurance companies and leveraging the power of cash, you can access

the highest-rated providers for your employees while saving money by paying the providers directly. Many employers are saving so much money that their employees benefit by having no deductibles, copays, or co-insurance, and they don't have to pay an employee contribution toward insurance premiums.

2. Companies can provide a benefit design incentive for employees to choose advanced primary care that gives employees access to a different front door to healthcare while experiencing a whole new model of primary care that's focused around the individual's goals and aspirations. Advanced primary care provides relationship-based healthcare that includes health coaching for continuous support through every part of life. It creates better health outcomes by preventing many serious health issues before they reach the need for more expensive procedures by helping individuals make better choices. Many employees can also receive access to mental health services, prescriptions, and more through their advanced primary care service at no additional cost. All of this is included in their monthly subscription cost.

3. When employees need healthcare services beyond primary care, they can access navigation partners through services such as White Glove by Orriant to help them find the highest quality care at the lowest prices and coordinate that care with their primary care provider. This third-party administrator handles paying all claims and gives employees access to all the 21 strategies described in this chapter.

4. Employees receive medical cash monthly in the form of an EBHRA account (more on these medical expense accounts in chapter 10) that's at their disposal to use to cover any

medical costs they'd like, whether that's purchasing dental or vision coverage, covering the cost of an urgent care visit, or paying for a prescription. Whatever money they don't use rolls over, and they get to keep the account even if they leave your company.

5. Employees who want to stick with the traditional system using a major insurance network provider (such as Cigna, Aetna, Blue Cross, or United Healthcare) may do so, either through a plan you provide or by purchasing their own coverage using your defined contribution dollars. You can even include the network of one of these large carriers through the Super Plan.

6. The Super Plan allows you to access other cost-saving services, such as fiduciary defense services that stop fraud and abusive charges like duplicate bills, as well as cost and quality transparency tools to ensure the best outcomes and prevent higher costs resulting from poor outcomes.

CHAPTER 10

The Aspirational Strategy for Small Employers

If your business is smaller and it doesn't make sense for you to self-fund your healthcare plan, I recommend a plan design using a *defined contribution strategy*, where your employees will play a larger role in creating their own healthcare benefits.

I see many employers make the mistake of thinking that if a solution isn't good for everyone, it must not be good for anyone. But that's a fallacy. Your HR department might be looking for a solution that works for every person, including someone who is an exception to the general rule, but in doing so, they end up buying a healthcare benefits program that doesn't work particularly well for everyone.

A defined contribution allows you to give your employees choice. They choose how to spend the benefit dollars you've set aside for them and they can buy what's best for their families. If they want to buy what they've always bought, let them, but give them the opportunity to buy something different.

My suggestion is not to put all your eggs in the same basket. I suggest you create four defined contribution funds—you can think of them as buckets of money—and let your employees decide how to use each of them:

1. Subscription-based primary care
2. Incentive for health coaching
3. Secondary and catastrophic care
4. Cash for medical expenses

The way you approach these four buckets, especially secondary and catastrophic care, can change depending on your plan design.

1. SUBSCRIPTION-BASED PRIMARY CARE

If the goal is to attract and retain top talent, the best way to keep your employees happy is through a strategy that allows them to choose where they spend their healthcare dollars. Put some money in a bucket dedicated to advanced primary care—your employees don't have to use it, but it's only for subscription-based advanced primary care. It's essentially saying, "Here's some money if you'll sign up for direct primary care. You can choose where to sign up, and we'll pay for it."

2. INCENTIVES FOR HEALTH COACHING

In addition to the primary care bucket, I recommend offering an incentive to get employees to take advantage of coaching. The best healthcare system in the world, Nuka, was built around coaching people.

Incentives are effective at engaging a large number of people to work with a coach. Getting people to adopt a new behavior can be challenging, but if you give people a significant enough incentive, in addition to paying for the coaching, you can get 50-90% of your employees and their spouses to work with a coach. The incentive helps get people past their inertia to get started doing something new.

Incentivizing this model will help your employees discover the benefits of relationship-based healthcare to help them live life to its fullest. The purpose is to support behavioral change and help them reach their aspirations. They get to decide what those aspirations are—you don't.

3. SECONDARY AND CATASTROPHIC CARE

The next basket is secondary and catastrophic care. This money can be used to purchase traditional insurance or something else, like a healthcare sharing program. Alternatively, if an employee would rather take that money (post-tax) to put toward their spouse's insurance plan, allow them to do so.

This ability to customize healthcare allows employees to save money by choosing what they need for their families. For example, many people would benefit more from a sharing program than an insurance plan, but most employees don't have the option to choose that unless their employer creates a strategy that allows them to. By using a defined contribution strategy, you give them the option to choose what's best for them.

For smaller employers without a self-funded plan, this bucket allows you to provide broader health coverage for your employees by giving them a fixed monthly amount to contribute to whatever healthcare plan they wish to purchase.

The new *individual coverage health reimbursement arrangement* (ICHRA) is a great option here. Employers contribute to an account that employees can use to purchase an individual plan of their choice. It separates the employer from the healthcare system. I recommend that employers who offer an ICHRA give their employees the option of taking the cash (post-tax) as an option. That way, they can put that cash toward another healthcare strategy if desired, such as helping to pay for a spouse's plan or purchasing a health-sharing program.

Whether you're self-funded or offering only a monthly defined contribution, it's important that the secondary and catastrophic care bucket is separate from the primary care bucket. While many options for secondary and catastrophic care (such as insurance plans) do include coverage for primary care, you want to encourage your employees to use subscription-based advanced primary care for two reasons:

1. To give them a better experience with healthcare

2. To stop feeding the dragon, the traditional healthcare system

Some individuals may still choose to access primary care through their insurance plan or opt out of advanced primary care. They have the right to do so, but you need to ensure they have the option and understand the choices they're making.

4. CASH FOR MEDICAL EXPENSES

The final bucket is cash for medical expenses, which can be placed in a variety of different tax-benefitted savings accounts for your employees to access as needed to pay for their healthcare needs.

Many employers are already using an FSA (flexible spending account), HSA (health savings account), or HRA (health reimbursement arrangement), but very few know about an EBHRA (excepted benefit health reimbursement arrangement). It's a type of HRA, and it's the only account that can be used to pay for both qualified medical expenses and excepted benefit premiums such as dental, vision, and supplemental policies.

This type of account has tremendous versatility and offers far more choice for employees. It can be used to pay for a supplemental plan like Aflac or a long-term care insurance plan. If they want to save up the money to pay for a cosmetic surgical procedure, they can do that or use it to cover the cost of holistic medical treatments. Employees can use it how they want to build their plans for their families.

I suggest employers use a vesting EBHRA and don't put any money into an HRA or an HSA until they've maxed out the EBHRA. With any health reimbursement arrangement (HRA or EBHRA), you as the employer fund the account and use it to reimburse employees for medical expenses—it's your money, not theirs.

Many employees prefer an HSA because it's their money in their own account, and they get to keep it when they leave. However, an EBHRA gives you the best of both options. You can design an HRA or an EBHRA to roll over from year to year and even follow an employee after they leave.

I recommend allowing your employees to vest the money in those accounts over time to encourage longevity—for example, 25% at two years, 50% at three years, 75% at four years and 100% at five years.

The beauty of the EBHRA is that it doesn't have to be tied to a certain plan.

An HSA has to be tied to a high-deductible plan and an HRA has to be tied to a group plan. The employee has to be on one of those plans in order to receive pre-tax cash from their employer.

The only requirement of an EBHRA is that the employer has to offer a group plan. The employee can choose not to be on the group plan and can still take the money post-tax and use it to join a health-sharing program, which makes an EBHRA much more flexible.

Tax Advantages

The cost of any medical services you provide your employees is tax-deductible, which includes the money you pay toward insurance premiums, primary care, specialist or catastrophic care, and any money you put into an EBHRA. However, any money that you offer as an incentive is *not* tax deductible. If you offer an incentive for your employees to receive health coaching, you can deduct the cost of the coaching but not the incentive.

Additionally, there are some health-sharing programs that meet requirements for offering coverage and that are tax-deductible. Usually, these are sharing programs that were grandfathered in when the Affordable Care Act was passed, but many sharing programs today do not meet these qualifications, so you should research the specific sharing program you're considering. Many of those grandfathered in were Christian ministry sharing programs.

PUTTING IT ALL TOGETHER

Now that we've covered the major components of an AH strategy for small employers, let's examine what it looks like in practice.

As a smaller employer, here's how I structure my benefits plan for my employees through the defined contribution strategy, which is also my personal health plan:

BUCKET 1: SUBSCRIPTION-BASED ADVANCED PRIMARY CARE

I set aside $64 every month for subscription-based advanced primary care. Personally, I spend a portion of that to purchase Nice Healthcare for me and my whole family, while some goes toward a single membership to a local urgent care network. That $64 per month covers the cost of both.

Through Nice Healthcare, I know my primary care provider, and my provider knows me—including my goals and aspirations. If I need to see my provider, I use their app to schedule a chat or a virtual call that same day or the next day. If it is urgent, I can talk to someone right away.

If I need to be seen in person, my provider schedules an appointment to see me in my home or office, usually the next day. My provider knocks on my front door, walks into my living room, and puts a stethoscope to my chest. If I need an X-ray, the X-ray machine and a technician come to my home. (I have had an X-ray done at my home twice now.) If I need labs done, my provider handles it when they come to see me. If I need counseling or physical therapy, they are both virtual and included for no extra cost.

I pay nothing additional for any of that because it's subscription based. I have access to over 500 medications for which I don't pay anything, and if I need a prescription that's outside the 500 prescriptions available, I leverage my Costco member discount program to get an extremely good deal on medications.

I have access to a number of urgent care facilities through a program called Medallus Medical here in Utah. If I have an emergency, such as a laceration, I can go to urgent care and pay $10, which I pull out of my EBHRA.

BUCKET 2: COACHING INCENTIVE

I offer coaching to my own employees as a part of our wellness program. They get money for working with one of our coaches on a regular basis.

I personally work with one of our coaches and it has been a great support to me in reaching some important goals in my life. The accountability I feel toward my coach because I speak to her regularly keeps me on track to make progress on my goals.

The extra cash my employees receive as incentive for working with a coach (or if they spend less than I give them in bucket 1 or bucket 3) is taxed and put on a debit card that they can use to buy anything they want. They know that the money on that debit card came from the choices they made through their benefits. It means a lot more to them that way than if it just went into their paycheck.

BUCKET 3: SECONDARY AND CATASTROPHIC CARE

For employees who have been with me for fewer than seven years, I put $300 per month into this third bucket. For employees who have been with me for more than seven years, I put in $400 per month.

My employees are offered a traditional group health insurance plan that has no participation requirements because it is community rated. As a result, I don't need 75% of all my employees to choose this plan in order to offer it. These kinds of plans are becoming more commonly available across the country due to the Affordable Care Act, and most small-employer plans are community rated.

This group plan offers my employees three options:

- A $2,000-deductible PPO (preferred provider organization) plan

- A $2,600-deductible PPO plan

- A $7,500-deductible HSA-qualified plan

The first plan is the most expensive and the third plan is the least expensive. The employee's portion of these plans, which comes out of their paycheck, varies based on whether they choose an employee-only or a family plan.

It is common for employers to put a larger amount of money into the secondary and catastrophic care bucket based on the following three categories: the need for family, two-party, and single coverage. Your company's situation will determine what amount is necessary.

If my employees want to take my $300 or $400 and put it toward a sharing program, I simply take taxes out and let them join whichever sharing program they choose. Some of my employees take the money post-tax and use it to help pay for their spouse's plan.

In the case of sharing programs, which are what most of my employees choose to join, the money I give them is more than enough, so I let them keep the difference. (More on sharing programs can be found on page 156.)

In fact, my employees who use a sharing program get money back whether they are buying single, two-party, or even whole-family coverage. Even those employees who get $400 per month and purchase a sharing program to cover their whole family only have to pay $39 a month out of their own pockets to be on one of the family sharing program options.

In my own case, I choose to use my defined contribution to purchase a sharing program called Sedera, through which I only spend an initial $500 on any health need. That means if I broke my ankle, it would cost me $500, and if there were ongoing complications that required many follow-up appointments over a number of years, I wouldn't have to keep paying for that treatment beyond that initial $500. The cost of anything I require for that health need is shared by my sharing community. Even if it's a multimillion-dollar case expanding over several years, $500 is all I ever pay. To me, that is certainly better than being on an insurance plan where deductibles start over every year.

I don't have a network I have to choose from. I can go to whichever provider I want because I pay for healthcare with cash and I access cash discounts for all healthcare services.

When you pay cash up front, many providers roll out the red carpet.

Providers love to get paid at the time of service. Through my sharing program, I also get expert second opinions, which can drive that initial $500 down even further. My sharing program has an arrangement with a network of surgical centers across the country and if I choose to use one of those, my initial $500 is waived.

BUCKET 4: CASH FOR MEDICAL EXPENSES

For my employees who have been with me for fewer than seven years, I put $125 into an EBHRA for them every month, which they can put toward a dental plan or any other excepted benefit plan, or it can roll over to the next year, if they don't use it toward premiums and don't have any qualified medical expenses during the year.

For my employees who have been with me for more than seven years, including myself, I put $175 into an EBHRA every month (the maximum amount allowed by the government at the time of printing).

I use that to cover my portion of my dental plan, and the rest gets set aside for when I need cash to pay for my portion of healthcare.

SUMMARY

As an employer, I spend $6,200 per employee per year, which is less than half the average cost of $13,800. And the most amazing part is that for most of my employees, 43% of that $6,200 is going into their pockets as either cash incentives or cash they can use for qualified medical expenses. As a result, my employees never want to leave me and I'm spending half as much as other employers.

I also pay for my employees to have access to an employee assistance program called Blomquist Hale, a mental health program with no limits on the number of sessions through which they can see a mental health professional face-to-face or virtually.

I set up this benefit strategy in order to give my employees access to the best possible healthcare while saving my company a lot of money on healthcare costs. I choose to place money in four buckets in order to give my employees the opportunity to choose what's best for them while incentivizing them to pick the options that will benefit us both the most.

If you have fewer than 50 employees and you're not required by law to give your employees healthcare benefits, there are many options you can take advantage of to attract and retain employees. Give them something they value, such as subscription-based advanced primary care and health coaching. You can offer a sharing program and if they want something else, they can go through their spouse, the government, or an individual plan to get health insurance. Aspirational healthcare is beneficial even to small employers, and investing in the well-being of your employees will pay off in the long run.

HEALTHCARE SHARING PROGRAMS

Also known as "health share" programs, sharing programs are independent cooperative groups that pool funds to cover the healthcare costs of their members. These programs operate differently from traditional insurance and usually cost significantly less. While historically these programs have been largely operated by religious organizations, this model has gained popularity and there are now many nonreligious programs available.

It's important to note that these programs are not insurance, and they come in many shapes and sizes. Some programs have a maximum payable amount, and when that maximum is reached, they won't pay any more toward your healthcare. Some have transparent financial data and others don't. Some require members to sign statements of religious belief, and many require an agreement to live a healthy lifestyle.

> The sharing program industry is still like the Wild West in many ways, so it's important to educate your employees about how to research sharing programs if you're giving them the option to use this strategy.

How do sharing programs work? A community agrees to share in each other's expenses to cover members' healthcare needs with an administrative organization managing the flow of money. They often leverage cash-pay strategies to keep costs low rather than using contracted networks.

If you're allowing your employees to use your money to pay for healthcare sharing programs, make sure you educate them about what they're getting and what to look for when choosing a program. Sharing programs may not be the best option for everyone, even though they work well for 80-90% of people.

Here are a few questions to help evaluate a sharing program:

- Is there a maximum payment amount, and if so, what is it?

- What is the statement of belief or lifestyle commitment required?

- What are the holes in the program? There may be areas they don't pay for, such as maternity care, infertility treatments, mental health, or prescriptions.

- How do claims get paid? Some programs send the member the money to pay the bill, and others pay healthcare providers on the member's behalf.

- How transparent is their financial data? Are members able to see how much money is in the pool?

- Is there an initial waiting period before the program will begin to share in paying for your healthcare needs? If there is, you may need to keep your traditional insurance plan during that waiting period.

Being aware of these limitations as an employer will also help you ensure your employees are getting their healthcare needs met.

At the time of this writing, the average amount that employers across America are paying for health insurance is $1,150 per employee per month, whereas a sharing program often costs less than half that much per month.

Misunderstandings About Aspirational Healthcare

Employees who want to purchase their own health insurance plans with their defined contribution will have to pay more than they would with a group rate through their employer.

One issue with the way the health insurance industry has developed is that the individual market is not rated like the group market. Pricing for a group market is based on spreading risk throughout the group, whereas for an individual, it's based on their family's personal risk.

For an individual shopping for their own insurance, a good broker can help them find a plan that won't cost them as much, but this is something employers need to be aware of. The last thing you want is to send your employees out to the wolves, applying online for individual plans, because navigating the industry is very difficult as an individual. If your employees are shopping for individual health insurance, one option is to go through the government at Healthcare.gov.

If you're giving your employees a defined contribution to purchase their healthcare, ensure you're educating them on their options and encourage them to use that contribution to buy something so they are protected from the costs of catastrophic healthcare problems.

CHAPTER 11

Steps for Implementing Aspirational Healthcare

Now that you understand the fundamental pieces of aspirational healthcare and how it benefits you and your employees, let's discuss how you can go about implementing it in your business. For many CEOs I've met, this is the most daunting part—changing what you do. It sounds like a pretty big headache, right? It doesn't have to be. In fact, implementing AH is simpler than you'd expect. I've broken it down into just a few key steps to follow.

If you desire a streamlined process, Orriant can help you navigate each of these steps to make implementing aspirational healthcare painless.

1. DEFINE YOUR PURPOSE FOR PURCHASING HEALTHCARE

As mentioned in chapter 1, the first step to begin implementing aspirational healthcare is defining your purpose for purchasing healthcare. Understanding your business objectives is foundational to building a plan that will help you achieve those objectives and shows you how to align the healthcare options you offer.

For most employers, their objectives can be categorized in four ways:

1. To attract and retain top talent
2. To create a healthy, productive workforce
3. To have employees be satisfied with their healthcare
4. To make healthcare more affordable

If these four objectives are not your objectives, define what they are for you.

My journey into aspirational healthcare came from my interest in continuous quality improvement (CQI). I asked, "Why aren't we asking the customer what they want?" You are the customer who is buying healthcare for your employees, so you should be asking yourself what you want.

> The first step in implementing a healthcare system that works for you is determining what you want.

2. MEASURE THE OUTCOMES

The next step is measuring the outcomes of your current healthcare options to see what is and isn't working well. Insist on having a dashboard that regularly updates you on the effectiveness of your investment.

Through my company's consulting services, called Premier Alignment Consulting, we help employers set up these monitors and dashboards. With this information, you'll be better equipped to customize a healthcare strategy that helps you reach your business objectives. Refer back to chapter 1 for a guide on how to do this.

Premier Alignment Consulting by Orriant also offers services to help companies put together a process to measure and create a system for continuous quality improvements. Sometimes it's as simple as an employee survey, and it can be expanded into a system to ask your employees questions on a regular basis so you see what is and isn't working and where there's room for improvement.

3. COLLABORATE WITH YOUR TEAM TO ALIGN YOUR GOALS

In order to save money on healthcare, you first must align the buying process to work toward your interests. That starts with your internal staff—usually HR—and your broker or benefit consultant. Ensure that they're incentivized to help you meet your business objectives above anything else.

Usually this requires you to find an independent broker who isn't working for a large brokerage firm and is able to sign a contract with you stating that they'll get paid based on how well they help you meet your goals rather than making a commission from an insurance company.

I have identified about 100 innovative advisors across the country who have all agreed to sign fee-based contracts with employers and align their incentives with the business objectives of their clients. I call this group Aspirational Healthcare Advisors. I am finding more advisors all the time. I invite them to a monthly virtual meeting where the group can share ideas.

We have created a certification process where these innovative advisors/consultants can become credentialed as certified aspirational healthcare advisors (CAAs). I recommend working with any consultant who is a CAA, as designated by Aspirational Healthcare, BLLC. Be sure to sign a fee-based contract with them and include incentives in the contract so they are aligned to help you reach your company goals.

Also ensure your HR employees' incentives are aligned with your business objectives for purchasing healthcare. This means measuring outcomes based on the data that matters to you, using the purposes you defined in the first step, and then making decisions based on that data. The same applies to other employees involved in the decision-making process around healthcare. Everyone on your team should be aligned with your goals and understand that the best way to achieve them is often not through traditional strategies they have deployed in the past.

4. DETERMINE DEFINED CONTRIBUTIONS—THE FOUR BUCKETS

Once you've found a broker who's willing to work for you and have aligned your internal team, it's time to evaluate your options for what you'll offer your employees.

If you're a larger employer, the best option is to self-fund your healthcare plan. Through Orriant, this is incredibly easy to implement using the Super Plan, which only requires you to sign one contract. Everything is already packaged together. See chapter 9.

If you're a smaller employer, there are many other resources to take advantage of, and I recommend the defined contribution strategy covered in chapter 10. Decide how much you will invest in each of the four buckets:

1. Subscription-based advanced primary care
2. Incentive for health coaching
3. Catastrophic care
4. Medical cash

Create resources for your employees to help them understand their options and determine what's best for their individual families.

If your broker is aligned with your interests, they will bring you plenty of options to help you find what will work best under your defined contribution strategy.

5. IDENTIFY TRUST CAPITAL

One of the most important factors in the success of implementing an aspirational healthcare plan is identifying and utilizing the *trust capital* within the organization. That is, knowing who within your organization inspires your employees' trust. Employees will be much more willing to participate if the changes come from someone they trust and believe has their best interests at heart. Who holds that trust capital is different for every organization, and it may not be immediately obvious. For more information on the role of trust in implementing aspiration healthcare, see chapter 12.

As part of Orriant's implementation process, we survey employees to determine who holds trust capital within the company. Is it HR, the CEO, the purchasing department secretary, or someone else? Who do they feel has their back?

Once these people have been identified, we bring them into the process of designing the new aspirational model. Get their feedback, make tweaks, and let them help you determine how you'll communicate and roll it out. This is immensely helpful in getting employee buy-in, and it's very important in helping you communicate effectively with your employees, especially in introducing the new healthcare benefits. The people who hold the trust capital should be the ones to communicate with the employees about their healthcare.

I recommend holding orientation meetings where these trusted individuals can introduce the new healthcare approach. However, communication must not stop there—it must be ongoing in order to continuously improve.

6. IMPLEMENT CONTINUOUS QUALITY IMPROVEMENT

Continuous quality improvement is one of the critical components that is missing from the current healthcare system—nobody is asking what they can do to improve the customer experience. But implementing continuous quality improvement for the way you purchase healthcare can make all the difference in saving money and meeting your business objectives. Continue to measure the outcomes of the changes you've made to discover whether it's working or not, then keep making adjustments. Even once you've developed a system that works well, keep measuring because you never know when you'll find more opportunities to improve it.

7. PROMOTE AND ADVERTISE THE NEW MODEL

When the Southcentral Foundation implemented the Nuka System of Care, they didn't just change the system and hope that everybody would like it. For the first 10 years, they did a lot of direct-to-consumer advertising. They produced their own newspaper that they mailed out to all 70,000 members talking about what they were doing and why they were doing it. They communicated their hope that their 70,000 people would change their understanding of healthcare's role in their lives. They started using the word customer-owner and explained that term. "You are the owner of your health journey. You own making your decisions. You own setting your goals. What we will do is provide you with informed expert options for you to choose between."

The Nuka System of Care committed to being immediately available with on-demand follow-up by text, phone, or email. This way, people don't have to invest half a day to take off work to attend an appointment, which discourages people from seeing their health-care providers.

This is also important for employers to do. Use today's popular communication tools to promote and advertise this new health-care model you are offering your team members. Highlight its advantages and how it will improve the lives of your employees and their family members.

A STORY OF HOW TO ADAPT ASPIRATIONAL HEALTHCARE

Aspirational healthcare is an incredibly adaptable model, and even within Orriant, each of our employees uses it a little bit differently to meet their needs. As an employer, it's important to remember that your employees know their own situations best and are capable of determining what's best for them. This is why choice is so important in aspirational healthcare.

One of my employees, Patrice, has a unique approach to her health benefits, which she's used to help cover a variety of needs including a cancer diagnosis. Here is how she tells her story:

> I've been unfortunate to have had many health issues, and blessed to have a husband who works for a large company with great health insurance. As a result, I get many of my needs taken care of through his insurance—the out-of-pocket costs throughout the year still add up between us and our two children. Because I had so many needs between my own health issues and needing care for

my kids, I set up a healthcare sharing program for myself (Sedera), and it has saved our family at least $50,000 in the four years that I've had it—that's even prior to my recent cancer diagnosis.

My family receives most of our healthcare through traditional insurance that we get through my husband's job, which covers the whole family. I'm the only person on my sharing program, and I pay $500 per issue or need. That cost doesn't start over every year—that $500 is a one-time cost for any single need. As long as I continue to have a claim on it, I don't keep paying.

In hindsight, I should have put the kids on the sharing program to limit how much we'd need to pay for them since one has needed ear surgery and the other broke his arm.

I'm running my cancer treatment needs through my traditional insurance first, and then my sharing program will share the cost of the rest of it. So far, they've paid for everything that insurance hasn't paid for.

It's been interesting to see how the billing has worked by going through insurance first. The healthcare system can charge my insurance whatever they want, and one of the genetic tests I needed for the cancer treatment was billed to insurance for $6,000. My portion of that was about $1,500, which my sharing program paid. After the initial screening mammogram, all of my needs related to the cancer are no longer considered preventive by my insurance, which means I have to pay for them. So the first screening, which was part of my annual, was covered, but everything after that I've had to pay for. Luckily, I already had my sharing program, so all I had to pay was $500.

My insurance was billed $122,000 for the surgery I needed, and it's likely all I'll need to pay is that $500. Because I ran the bills through my insurance first, I didn't have to do any research to find out what the cash price would be. As a result, the most my sharing program would have to pay is my maximum out of pocket on my insurance policy.

CHAPTER 12

How to Avoid Potential Risks

Aspirational healthcare is gaining momentum in the U.S. and throughout the world as more people discover how much better healthcare can be. More employers are moving toward self-funded healthcare plans with an aspirational model not just to provide better healthcare at a lower cost, but also to protect themselves from liability.

Beyond helping you reach your business objectives for purchasing healthcare, aspirational healthcare has the potential to help organizations avoid liability by meeting requirements for new and developing governmental regulations in regard to employers' responsibilities for their employees' healthcare.

In 1974, when the Employee Retirement Income Security Act (ERISA) was passed, the government determined that businesses have a fiduciary obligation to their employees when they invest their money in pension plans. Since companies were handling employees' money and controlling how it would show up in their retirement, they had a fiduciary duty to manage it responsibly. Of course, that created a significant amount of liability for companies and their CEOs. As a result, employers began implementing 401(k)s to replace pension plans, which allowed the employees to be responsible for their own money and choose how to invest it.

More recently in 2021, the Consolidated Appropriations Act (CAA) was passed, which applied similar language to the healthcare benefits that employers provide for their employees. The decisions that business leaders make about the healthcare they purchase directly impacts the cost of healthcare for their employees in terms of premiums, copays, deductibles, and co-insurance.

As long as your employees are responsible for paying any portion of their healthcare plan, you are acting as a fiduciary for them in that role. Your decisions as an employer affect how your employees spend their money, so you have a fiduciary responsibility to them. Now, the Department of Labor is doing audits and fining companies that don't have a good fiduciary duty plan in place in regard to buying healthcare.

But there's more than just fines from the Department of Labor at risk here—employees are allowed to file class-action lawsuits against their employers for a lack of fiduciary responsibility, and they can go not only after your business, but also your personal assets as the CEO. In fact, even though the CAA was passed pretty recently, there are already several lawsuits underway.

The U.S. government is aware that healthcare costs have skyrocketed to unmanageable levels, and the CAA is an attempt to help control those costs through employers. And they're not entirely on the wrong track, either—employers *do* have the ability to influence the cost of healthcare through our purchasing decisions. We have the ability to make a difference by providing better, less expensive healthcare to our employees, holding the healthcare industry accountable by creating alignment with what matters to us, and measuring the right outcomes.

As an employer, the CAA requires that you have a documented system in place to identify where your healthcare dollars are going and to determine whether those costs are prudent and reasonable. But the reality is that it's very difficult to track those things, especially with insurance companies as an intermediary. The healthcare industry is fraught with waste and fraud, which insurance companies do little to nothing to stop. And just about every employer out there is not going to measure up to compliance with the new standards.

Basically, the CAA states that if you, an employer offering benefits, are requiring an employee to pay anything toward those benefits—copays, deductibles, premiums, etc.—you're making decisions on how their money is being spent, and therefore you're a fiduciary.

As a fiduciary, you have an obligation to your employees to ensure you're making good decisions with their money.

Aspirational healthcare can help address some of this fiduciary responsibility by dramatically lowering or even eliminating employee contributions to healthcare. If your plan doesn't require your employee to pay anything, you've reduced your fiduciary responsibility significantly. By offering innovative plans, you can limit your fiduciary risk.

I believe that the CAA has the potential to rein the healthcare industry back into control if employers take the opportunity to move in the right direction and create alignment within the industry through an aspirational model.

In fact, CEOs have the power to do so while spending less and getting better health outcomes for their employees.

Aspirational healthcare can contribute to a process that will help you meet the requirements of the CAA to protect yourself from liability of both fines and lawsuits.

To learn more about the CAA requirements for employers, read *Understanding Your Fiduciary Responsibilities Under a Group Health Plan*, a guide that provides an overview of the basic responsibilities applicable to group health plans. I have provided a link to this government document at the end of this chapter.

The Employee Retirement Income Security Act (ERISA) sets standards for fiduciaries, those who manage employee benefit plans and their assets. ERISA covers employment-based group health plans that provide medical care coverage, including hospitalization, prescription drugs, vision, and dental. This applies whether the plan uses funds in a plan trust, insurance, or self-funding. I highly recommend reading more about your responsibilities as an employer for the group health plan you offer.

As a CEO, you're considered a fiduciary, which means that you're personally responsible and a lawsuit can come after your personal assets. However, people considered fiduciaries aren't limited to just the CEO. Anyone with discretion over the plan can be considered a fiduciary and is subject to standards of conduct on behalf of the employees who use the plan and their beneficiaries.

Here are some of your responsibilities as a fiduciary of your employees' healthcare plans:

- Acting solely in the interest of plan participants and their beneficiaries, with the exclusive purpose of providing benefits to them

- Carrying out your duties prudently

- Following the plan documents (unless inconsistent with ERISA)

- Holding plan assets (if the plan has any) in trust

- Paying only reasonable plan expenses

As a fiduciary, if you don't follow these standards of conduct, you may be personally liable for any losses to the healthcare plan or to restore any profits made through improper use of the plan's assets as a result of your actions.

As you can see, these requirements may not always be straightforward in their interpretation, so acting with fiduciary responsibility requires expertise. For most CEOs, that will mean hiring a fiduciary coach with professional knowledge to carry out these duties and document decisions and the basis for those decisions to protect themselves from liability. Orriant can help you find the resources you need to meet these duties.

AH COULD HELP YOU SIDESTEP CLASS ACTION LAWSUITS

Several class-action lawsuits have already been started against employers for failure to comply with CAA. These are lawsuits against major employers. I suspect we'll soon hear about many more.

The reality is that almost no employers are currently compliant with the CAA. Most are not taking it as seriously as they should be, and likely they won't until enough class action lawsuits are filed.

Smaller companies are not at as high a risk as big companies because most large law firms will want to go after household name brands, and it's the large law firms that will drive the class action lawsuits.

Many lawyers known for class action lawsuits, including those involving 401(k)s, health benefits, and pensions, have begun using social media to reach out to employees of certain large companies to find potential plaintiffs.

That's not to say that smaller companies shouldn't also be concerned. All employers offering benefits have fiduciary duty.

One of the ways to avoid some of the risks associated with your fiduciary duty is to offer more options to your employees. That was what happened with pension plans—employers began offering 401(k)s where employees had choice in where to invest their money.

Orriant's Super Plan is one of the only plan design options that helps employers meet all their fiduciary obligations. It was created with that purpose in mind.

HOW CAN BUSINESSES MEET CAA REQUIREMENTS?

Documenting your processes is the first step in proving your responsibility, but there are a number of things you should consider as you make decisions to protect your employees' interests.

Let's start with fees for services, which are paid from the assets within your healthcare plan. The law requires that fees charged to a plan must be "reasonable," which isn't specifically defined. You need a strong understanding of the fees being charged and the services provided and then you should monitor them closely.

The first step is to carefully evaluate fees when selecting a health-care service provider. Compare estimates and ask what is included within the estimate and what's not included—sometimes services are bundled into one fee and sometimes they're charged separately.

A service provider can be anyone paid for any kind of healthcare-related services. These include but are not limited to the following:

- Broker

- Third-party administrator

- Insurance company

- Reinsurance company (if self-funded)

- Captive groups

- All point solutions

- Primary care providers

It's best to establish a formal review process with service providers that you use to check in regularly and review whether you want to continue using their services or look for a replacement.

There are many other elements of the ERISA requirements that you should be aware of, and I highly recommend reading through *Understanding Your Fiduciary Duties Under a Group Health Plan* (https://www.dol.gov/sites/default/files/ebsa/about-ebsa/our-activities/resource-center/publications/understanding-your-fiduciary-responsibilities-under-a-group-health-plan.pdf) to get a full picture of the requirements. It's an easy-to-understand guide that will give you a great start to meeting compliance standards with the CAA.

This all may seem like a lot to keep track of, but it's worth it. The good news is that developing processes to meet CAA compliance and approaching your fiduciary responsibilities genuinely can help you save money on healthcare while helping to transform

176 MAKE HEALTHCARE WORK FOR YOU

the healthcare system and providing much better healthcare for your employees.

What the government is asking employers to do through the CAA is very similar to what aspirational healthcare already accomplishes—setting goals for healthcare, measuring to see if your healthcare solutions are achieving them, and working toward better healthcare at a better price for the sake of both your business and your employees.

CHAPTER 13

Overcome Common Challenges

One of the biggest hurdles most CEOs face in implementing aspirational healthcare is a resistance to change, from the executive all the way down to the individual employee level. Change can seem hard, but staying with the status quo is simply not an option for many employers. Restructuring your entire healthcare system, not to mention learning about a new system, can be daunting. In the past, you've simply shopped for an existing system, and even though aspirational healthcare can save you money and create better results, it does take some work to get it started.

I hope that in reading this book you've come to understand the benefits that AH can provide to your business and your employees. These benefit programs are well worth the initial effort to implement them, and that implementation does not have to be as difficult as you might expect.

Once they understand the benefits of aspirational healthcare, most CEOs are ready to make the change, at which point the challenge shifts to getting employees on board. On an individual level, employees may also be resistant to change—they're familiar with their insurance and know how it works, and perhaps they have a good relationship with their current doctor and don't like the idea of having to change.

Your employees may also be confused about the new healthcare system, especially since aspirational healthcare is so different from the traditional insurance-based model. That confusion can lead to worries about how they'll get their healthcare needs met or what their costs will be.

The good news is that costs under the aspirational model are more controllable because of the ability to shop around for the best prices and outcomes. Patients aren't stuck with paying whatever price the provider dictates, which often is unknown until after the services have been rendered. It also goes a long way toward preventing fraud such as price gouging, surprise billing, and upcoding, which all exploit patients and their employers for more money than they should be charged.

Helping your employees understand these factors as well as the aspirational healthcare system as a whole goes a long way toward creating buy-in, and it's why your communication strategy is a vital part of your implementation process.

IMPROVE COMMUNICATION AND IDENTIFY TRUST CAPITAL

The reality is that no matter how strong your workplace culture is, many employees do not trust their employers to have their best interests in mind. They may perceive any changes to their benefits plans to simply be about cutting costs. A dramatic change like this one can set alarm bells off in their heads, even if you really have their best interests at heart.

One of the first steps in implementing an aspirational healthcare plan, as described in chapter 11, is to identify who within the organization holds the most trust capital. This might be multiple people, and they play a critical role in successful implementation because they're needed to create employee buy-in. Often these people are not the top executives, but people with whom the employees interact regularly.

The people who hold the trust capital serve as your primary communicators, so they must have a strong understanding of the new model in order to help your employees understand how it works and how they'll benefit from it.

> ## An employee who is confused will not choose to use your new healthcare plan—they will stick with what they know because it feels safe.

In communicating the new benefits to employees, stress not only how they can benefit from it, but also the fact that they have a choice—they can stick with their current healthcare strategy if they want to. You are expanding their benefits, not reducing them, and incentivizing them to take care of their health with a new, better system.

Stories can be particularly effective in illustrating how the new model works and helping employees understand it. Stories can connect on an emotional level so employees can envision how it can work for them. Be transparent about its benefits and its drawbacks in order to help individuals make the best choices for their families.

PROMOTE EMPLOYEE EDUCATION AND INVOLVEMENT

Depending on how you set up your plan, aspirational healthcare may also require employees to be more involved in their healthcare up front. While certain plan designs require very little from employees, others rely upon the employee finding and purchasing their own healthcare. In such cases, they need to be willing to do some research and take part in coordinating their healthcare.

Whatever your plan design looks like, employee education is a vital part of implementation in order to help everyone get the most out of their healthcare.

The education you provide should include helping employees understand how to use their aspirational healthcare benefits and how they benefit from the AH model.

For companies that don't want their employees to have to navigate the healthcare system on their own, we created the White Glove full-service concierge program. Part of the purpose of White Glove is to make using an aspirational healthcare model as easy as possible. It gives you a partner to navigate your healthcare, your personal concierge whom you know and you can call directly, and you can trust them to hold your hand through whatever you're experiencing.

For smaller employers who are using a defined-contributions plan design, employees will need to be more involved in research and coordination. It's up to them how they will spend their defined contributions, which may mean searching for and purchasing their own healthcare plan, researching and coordinating their own care, and even handling billing issues. It's something that not every person is willing to do, and that's why choice and education are both so important.

Both employer and employee need to be prepared to invest some time in educating themselves in order to make good choices for their healthcare. Those who are willing to put in the effort can experience a much better model of healthcare, but it requires opting in. Of course, some people will find it too complicated and will stick with what they've always done, but for those who are willing to put in a little effort, they can save a significant amount on their healthcare and have more agency in the process. The key is to communicate how they will achieve those savings with the AH approach and the benefits they'll get beyond what their current plan offers.

Your employee education should also include details on the options available to purchase using your defined contribution, such as government exchange insurance policies (Healthcare.gov), individual insurance policies, and sharing programs. Offer them help in choosing something that fits for their family and ensure they understand their choices and how they can save money by learning how to use the tools available to them.

If you have more than 50 employees on your health plan, the Super Plan offers you an easy way to implement an aspirational healthcare plan with very little effort.

If you have under 50 employees on your health plan, aspirational healthcare is a more creative approach to meeting your healthcare needs, but it does require more decision-making on both the part of the CEO and the individual employees. This model invites you to be a shopper, to engage in the process rather than being passive about it. As a result, you'll save money and have better outcomes, but you have to be willing to put in some effort.

Because choice is one of the pillars of aspirational healthcare, you're not forcing your employees into anything, only encouraging them to take a different front door into the healthcare system. They can choose to keep doing what they've always done.

Educating your employees isn't entirely up to you as their employer, either. One of the major pieces of aspirational healthcare is the role of a coach. The coach serves as an educational resource for employees and is also someone in their corner to advocate for them. Your personal coach can direct you to resources, be a safe space to discuss concerns you have, and help you determine next steps.

MANAGE RISKS AND UNDERSTAND LIMITATIONS

As you've come to understand by now, AH is not a specific healthcare plan so much as an overall model with many ways it can be implemented. Some of those plan designs carry more risks than others, but all of them give employees more choice in their healthcare and can save a significant amount of money for both employees and employers.

What's important is to be aware of potential weaknesses in the plan design, educate your employees so they can make informed choices, and mitigate risks wherever you can.

LIMITATIONS OF REFERENCE-BASED PRICING

For example, if you decide to use reference-based pricing as we discussed in chapter 8, it can save a lot of money, but the drawback is that it can put your employees in the middle of a battle between you and the healthcare provider. Because more companies have begun to use this model to save money, some hospitals are saying that they won't see anyone who is using reference-based pricing. However, you can work around these risks by building your plan to accommodate them, and you should never choose reference-based pricing if you're not willing to pay 100% of the billed balance.

LIMITATIONS OF SHARING PROGRAMS

If you're directing your employees toward sharing programs, you need to be aware of the benefits and drawbacks that sharing programs tend to come with and give your employees tools to help them make an informed choice. For someone with a chronic health condition who has expensive pharmaceutical needs, a sharing program is likely not a good option because most sharing programs pay for pharmaceuticals based on a need for 90 days and won't keep paying for medications for chronic conditions. For example, if someone has MS, they should probably be on an insurance plan that will cover their medications because there are some highly effective MS medications, but they are very expensive. Another example is that most sharing programs limit their sharing for some mental health services, so someone with a serious psychiatric condition that may require regular hospitalizations would not be suited to a sharing program.

One of the things I like best about many of the sharing programs is that if your community has more medical expenses than can be covered with the members' monthly contributions, everyone is asked to contribute more. You don't have a locked-in contribution every month. I have been on a sharing program for many years and have never experienced a mid-year increase, but it could happen. I have only seen an increase at the end of the year once. With insurance, you can expect an increase every year.

Why is that a good thing? Well, if my sharing program needed to keep increasing my contribution and it became as expensive as insurance, I could always jump from a sharing program to an insurance plan during open enrollment each year. As long as my sharing program will pay for any catastrophic health expenses I may experience and the cost of participating in that sharing program is less than half the cost of a health insurance plan, I will stay on a sharing program.

For many families, it often comes down to comparing their premiums, out-of-pocket costs, and deductibles to the cost of a sharing program and what it will pay for. Generally speaking, sharing programs are half as expensive as insurance, which is fantastic for most families.

LIMITATIONS OF SUBSCRIPTION-BASED PRIMARY CARE

If you're paying for subscription-based advanced primary care and offering incentives for your employees to participate in coaching, many of their needs will be taken care of before insurance or a sharing program is even needed to pay for the costs of specialists or catastrophic care. But keep in mind that not all advanced primary care companies offer the same benefits, and while some come with amazing value for the price of your subscription, many only cover the cost of the doctor alone. That means if you need blood work done or an x-ray, for example, those costs will be additional. It's best to shop for one that has those features included in the subscription cost. A good advanced primary care plan will minimize the costs you have to run through your healthcare coverage, which may require you to pay a deductible, copay, and co-insurance.

While there's a great deal to learn about the various options available and their benefits and limitations, you don't have to figure it out on your own. In fact, your role is simply to define your objectives for purchasing healthcare, measure the outcomes, and create alignment to achieve those objectives. Your benefits consultant and human resources department, if aligned to work for your goals, should help you navigate all of these details. Orriant can also guide you through every step of implementation.

Overall, aspirational healthcare carries fewer risks to both you as an employer and to your employees than the traditional healthcare system because it reduces costs, creates better health outcomes, and prioritizes choice so that everyone is able to pick what's best for their situation.

CHAPTER 14

CEOs Must Lead the Healthcare Revolution

We're all aware that the current U.S. healthcare system is broken, with costs continuously shooting upward while health outcomes only seem to get poorer with many chronic diseases on the rise. But we aren't powerless to fix it. In fact, as a CEO, you have the ability to change it. Make healthcare work for you!

CEOs must be the ones to spearhead the healthcare transformation in the U.S. and lead the movement toward a system of care that puts the customer first. I firmly believe that we can do this together. I see the level of hatred CEOs hold for the current healthcare system, the way it exploits both employers and employees; it's a keg of dynamite just waiting to go off. Once a large enough number of employers begin to save money and offer better healthcare through aspirational healthcare, it won't take long for the rest of the country to adapt.

This kind of change has been achieved in the U.S. before, and it can happen again. After World War II, the IRS offered tax deductions to employers to offer healthcare benefits to their employees, and within 10 years, the majority of Americans were on their employers' insurance plans. It didn't take long because it provided people with a preferable option. I think the same thing can happen with aspirational healthcare. The evidence shows that it works—it saves money while providing a better service, and all we need is enough momentum to change the traditional way employers approach healthcare. In fact, that movement has already started, with many jumbo employers adopting an aspirational healthcare model.

What likely keeps health insurance executives up at night is the thought that the American people will eventually discover they provide little value.

They've misled the public, quietly diverting money in ways that often go unnoticed. Their greatest concern is that people might one day realize what's really happening.

With rising costs across the board, many families are looking at their expenses to determine what does or doesn't provide them with value. And it's hard to overlook the fact that you pay thousands of dollars a year for a service that you can barely even use until you've met your deductible—which might also be in the thousands of dollars—just to get partial coverage of your expenses. You pay hundreds on your premium every month, and then occasionally go to the doctor where you pay a copay, and then you get a bill in the mail a while later asking for more money after your co-insurance has kicked in—and that will only kick in *after* you've met your deductible. You just keep paying and paying. Employers and their employees are beginning to ask, "What am I getting in return for my money?" The system is expensive, confusing, and complicated, and many people don't understand it.

The majority of large employers are already self-funded, but they're handing their employees networks of primary care providers that are owned by hospitals, and they're just feeding the dragon. They're not applying the strategies of aspirational healthcare to save money. They're not addressing the primary care problem, they're not steering their employees to better and less expensive providers, and they're not bypassing the games played by PBMs. Most of all, they're not applying a long-term strategy to improve the health of their workforce and reduce the need for treatment of chronic diseases.

But the employers who are applying aspirational healthcare strategies are not only paying half as much for healthcare, but they're creating a healthier, happier workforce. An added bonus is they are building a better workplace culture that fosters loyalty by investing in the health and aspirations of the employees.

As I mentioned early in the book, the waste in the U.S. healthcare industry is equal to the entire gross domestic product of Russia—I'd like to see that waste stripped out of the healthcare industry and go toward better uses. Imagine the problems we could solve if that money went into everyone's pockets.

THE OPPORTUNITIES OF THE FUTURE

The rise of the aspirational healthcare model's popularity will continue to increase the options available for healthcare services, from direct primary care to coaching and even sharing programs. As demand for these services rises, the market will rise to meet them, and I've already seen it happening.

One of the big questions I've often received is, "How can there be enough primary care providers for everyone to access direct primary care when there's already a shortage of primary care providers across the country? How could a form of primary care where providers only have around 600-1,000 patients possibly be viable when currently they're each trying to see 2,000-4,000? How could you even educate that many primary care providers to fill the gap?"

These are actually simple questions to answer. Almost any primary care provider you talk to right now doesn't like the system they're in. They don't like having to see 30-40 people a day, wrestle with insurance to get their patient's needs met and get paid for their services, and feed the dragon of the healthcare system where they're incentivized to fill up hospital beds and make as much money for the administration as possible. Fortunately, aspirational healthcare is the opposite of that.

We're not trying to get more physicians into bad jobs. Instead, we're creating an environment through advanced primary care where people *want* to work—where they can do their job at the top of their abilities, make more money by not having to wrestle with insurance companies, and truly care for their patients. We're creating an option that's better than the traditional system.

And you know what? It's already working. There's been an exodus from the healthcare industry as healthcare professionals have wrestled with burnout under the traditional system. But direct primary care offers them an option to continue practicing their profession on better terms. And it includes more than just physicians—people like physician assistants and nurse practitioners, a rapidly expanding professional sector of the healthcare industry, are also jumping in on direct advanced primary care.

When there's demand, the supply will adapt and grow. What we have under the current traditional system is a demand for a lousy job that nobody wants to be in, which is why there's a shortage.

I remember over 20 years ago imagining that someday we'd be able to look at a watch on our wrists and get information about our health. That exists now. Technology has grown a great deal in my lifetime, and it's made some great strides for healthcare. I also now have quick access to my primary care provider through a phone call or a text.

Part of how the Nuka System of Care was so successful, despite covering a large number of communities spread across many small villages in Alaska, is that they utilized technology well. They do a lot of care over the phone, and they train assistants—such as physician assistants, nursing assistants, or pharmacy assistants—within the small villages to carry out much of the healthcare at a local level while being supported by medical doctors through technology. This way, the doctors only travel when needed.

Shining a light on what the Nuka System of Care is doing is the best way to revolutionize healthcare. If they can do it, we can figure it out too. I see technology and quick access to healthcare flourishing, because it makes healthcare more accessible. You don't have to take a whole day off work to see the doctor when you can do a video call.

CHANGING THE CULTURE THROUGH HEALTHCARE

Imagine that the entire U.S. healthcare system really was like the Nuka System of Care, and healthcare was about helping people reach their dreams. What impact would that have on the country's physical health, mental and emotional health, and productivity? It would restore faith in the American dream because it would literally be helping people achieve it.

My journey into aspirational healthcare began by managing psychiatric hospitals and watching people wind up having major psychiatric events, including suicide. I always wondered, "Why does someone have to be diagnosed as mentally ill to have someone in their corner helping them be successful in life?"

If someone is mentally ill, they get a therapist who helps them be more successful in all parts of life. But shouldn't we be offering that kind of support to everybody? What if we took a preventive approach not only to physical health but also to mental health? Imagine everyone having a partner to help them navigate life's challenges, to be emotionally well, and to have great family relationships? What would the world look like? I think it would be a friendlier, happier place overall. We could reduce the rate of suicides, mental illness, chronic disease, and possibly even abuse and domestic violence.

Heart disease is the number one killer in the U.S., and we know how to eliminate it entirely through preventive care.

So why don't we? Because it isn't profitable to do so. One of the most sophisticated ways to evaluate heart risks is the multifunction cardiogram (MCG), which doesn't require any invasive procedures. By screening people regularly, we could identify people who are at risk and ensure they get optimal medical therapy to address and reverse heart disease. If we included that as part of primary care, we could prevent heart disease as a whole. We could screen for pre-diabetes when it's still reversible, and we could better assess risks for cancer and screen for it to make sure it's addressed early on.

But if you find any cardiology program and ask how many people they've worked with who didn't already have a heart attack, the answer is always going to be no one. Their programs are designed to prevent the second heart attack—not the first. That's because primary care providers are only given 10 minutes with each patient to talk about their current symptoms and prescribe medication or referrals.

By changing the way we approach primary care, we can transform the health of the nation, both mentally and physically, and that starts by offering your employees advanced primary care and coaching and incentivizing them to use it.

COLLABORATING TO CREATE THE FUTURE

Aspirational healthcare requires the involvement of CEOs to be successful. That doesn't mean you have a second job—on the contrary, your involvement need only be at the highest level as the visionary and driver of change.

CEOs bring strategic advantages to healthcare initiatives, but the majority of the work can be taken care of by your team. You can choose to what extent you are involved. The only things you must be involved in to some degree are defining your objectives for purchasing healthcare and monitoring to ensure those objectives are being met. That could simply mean reviewing the information once a year so you're aware of whether the steps your team is taking are working.

Your job is to insist on alignment. Choose your objectives, measure them, and insist that those driving the healthcare system are recognized and rewarded for helping you accomplish your goals.

Insist on having a regularly updated dashboard that lets you know whether you are getting what you want from your investment in healthcare benefits.

It's simple—the problem is that you're not already doing it. Many CEOs think of healthcare as a purchase to be made that can be delegated to someone else. They don't feel they have the power to change it, so they don't try. But you aren't powerless against the healthcare system—in fact, you're the only one who can change it. And the best part is *it's easy!*

Implementing the aspirational model doesn't have to be your responsibility. You only need to understand it well enough to convey your objectives and have your team set it up. Be the driver by informing people of what's important.

The person you should have choosing your healthcare options and building your healthcare strategies should be aligned to monitor the outcomes in order to reach your goals. They should be insisting that their consultant is aligned to help them reach your goals as well. The best benefits manager would be an innovator, open to change, and not stuck in the old system where everyone is comfortable.

When your team—including your HR department, benefits manager, and benefits consultant—are aligned with your objectives, you need only hold them accountable. That's all it takes for you to begin leading the healthcare revolution by providing better healthcare to your employees at half the price.

TOGETHER WE CAN TRANSFORM HEALTHCARE

I truly believe in the potential of aspirational healthcare to transform the culture of the healthcare industry as a whole by making people healthier in every aspect of life.

My goal for Orriant is to shine a bright light on the
best healthcare system in the world. The world I want to create
is one where people think of healthcare as a partner to
help them do what they want to do.

We've already begun to awaken a big movement. I want to continue to drive that movement and facilitate companies who are implementing aspirational healthcare for their employees.

Of course, aspirational healthcare is going to save you and your employees money, and it will help you reach your business objectives, but it's also part of a larger movement to make things better for everyone.

Aspirational healthcare has already seen phenomenal success where it's been implemented, and we can keep that growing together. The more people who learn about it, the more people it can reach and benefit. It truly has the power to transform not just businesses but people's individual lives and cultures as a whole.

I mentioned in the introduction that Southcentral Foundation has had organizations and countries from around the world come to Alaska to learn about the Nuka System of Care, and there's little that I find more energizing than that. This solution extends beyond the U.S.—it's a movement that can make change on a global level.

Just a few of the countries who have come to Alaska to learn from Nuka include Norway, Singapore, the Polynesian Islands, the Cherokee Nation, several Canadian provinces, and other Native American tribes. The way each of them is implementing what they've learned is somewhat different, but it shows that these principles can apply on a very broad scale.

The Cherokee in North Carolina have done a remarkable job of replicating the Nuka model for their population, and they're getting some great outcomes. Singapore built a part of their healthcare system around Nuka's relationship-based model and they are applying it for people with high-risk, chronic conditions.

As aspirational healthcare becomes more well known, it can make a difference for more people around the world. This is the future of healthcare. And you can join the movement by helping me shine a light on the best healthcare system in the world.

The more employees benefit from aspirational healthcare, the more they will tell their friends and family about the other options that exist. And if you, as a CEO, haven't taken the time to think about your objectives for purchasing healthcare in the past, it's likely that many of your peers haven't either. Start the discussion around the healthcare revolution by letting people know that a system already exists that provides better outcomes at half the cost.

Join the movement to create a healthcare system built around meeting the needs of the customer that produces better health outcomes, helps us reach our goals, and is affordable for employers and employees alike.

CEOs must lead the charge, and together we can create the change that's needed to transform healthcare.

HEALTHCARE INDUSTRY TERMS

ACA (Affordable Care Act): The Affordable Care Act (ACA) of 2010 created a requirement that, in most cases, 85% of what insurance companies collect in premiums has to go toward paying healthcare claims. If less goes toward claims, the insurance company has to return the money to the customers.

ACL (anterior cruciate ligament): A ligament in the knee that commonly is injured and requires surgery to repair or reconstruct.

ADHD (attention deficit/hyperactivity disorder): A developmental disorder marked by persistent symptoms of inattention and/or hyperactivity and impulsivity. See https://www.nimh.nih. gov/health/topics/attention-deficit-hyperactivity-disorder-adhd

AH (aspirational healthcare): Originally developed by the Southcentral Foundation in Alaska and called the Nuka System of Care, aspirational healthcare is a relationship-based system of healthcare built around the customer.

APC (advanced primary care): A subscription-based model of primary care where a patient has a direct relationship with their provider and access to their care whenever they need it. Services are often delivered virtually or in the patient's home. Also called direct primary care (DPC).

ASC (ambulatory surgery center): Outpatient surgery centers separate from hospitals that provide same-day surgery services.

ASO (administrative services only) provider: Usually associated with an insurance company, an ASO provider provides customer service for health insurance claims and member management, and connects customers to the services offered through the insurance company.

BUCA (Blue Cross, United, Cigna, or Aetna): The four big health insurance companies that dominate the traditional health insurance industry.

CAA (certified aspirational healthcare advisor): A health insurance broker who is committed to aligning their compensation with the success of the company. Not to be confused with a certified anesthesiologist assistant or a certified accounting analyst. See also the Consolidated Appropriations Act.

CAA (Consolidated Appropriations Act): In 2021, the Consolidated Appropriations Act was passed by Congress, which applied a fiduciary responsibility to the healthcare benefits that employers provide for their employees.

Cancer centers of excellence: A program that provides patients with an expert second opinion from a global cancer center of excellence, due to the high probability of incorrect diagnoses and treatments. Because of its complexity and pathology, over 70% of first diagnoses and/or prescribed therapies for cancer are wrong. These programs increase the odds of obtaining the right treatment in a shorter period of time.

CAT scan (computerized axial tomography, a.k.a. a CT scan, computed tomography): An imaging procedure that uses a computer linked to an X-ray machine to take a series of detailed pictures inside the body, potentially along with a dye that is administered to improve contrast. A three-dimensional image of the patient results, which can be used for easier identification of basic structures as well as abnormalities such as tumors. See https://www.nibib.nih.gov/science-education/science-topics/computed-tomography-ct

Coaching vendors: Vendors who partner with many of the subscription-based advanced primary care providers to integrate coaching into the primary care clinical team, just like the Nuka System of Care does.

Consumer engagement tool vendors: Vendors who supply consumer tools that make accessing healthcare services simple, which can include tools like an AI-powered employee benefits app that can provide real-time, personalized answers on benefits coverage, treatment options, and preventive care tips.

CQI (continuous quality improvement): W. Edwards Deming's method for continuous quality improvement is a system based around four simple steps:

- Identify who is your customer.
- Identify what delights your customer.
- Measure the processes that most impact delighting your customer.
- When you find variance in a process, get the people closest to the process to improve it and eliminate the variance.

DPC (direct primary care): See APC (advanced primary care). Direct primary care providers are medical professionals (usually physicians, physician assistants, or nurse practitioners) who develop relationships with their patients and are paid to keep them well.

EBHRA (excepted benefit health reimbursement arrangement): A type of HRA that is funded by employers for employees to use. It is more flexible than an HRA and can be used to pay for both qualified medical expenses and excepted benefit premiums such as dental, vision, and supplemental policies. These accounts can be set up to carry over from year to year and even to become owned by the employees and follow them if they leave the company. See https://www.agentbrokerfaq.cms.gov/s/article/What-is-an-excepted-benefit-Health-Reimbursement-Arrangement

ERISA (Employee Retirement Income Security Act): A 1974 law that establishes employers' fiduciary responsibility in regard to their employees' pension plans.

FSA (flexible spending account or arrangement): A special savings account offered by employers and funded with an employee's pretax money. Employers may contribute to these accounts but are not required to. Funds can be used to reimburse employees for certain out-of-pocket healthcare costs. These funds are limited to $3,200 per year per employer. FSA funds may carry over with special grace period limits and in general are designed to be used in the current year. Funds not used by the end of the grace period are lost. See https://www.healthcare.gov/have-job-based-coverage/flexible-spending-accounts/

Hazardous prescription protection vendors: Personalized support from a clinical pharmacist can make sure medications are working their best and reduce side effects for your members. These vendors provide review by a pharmacist of the patients and medications being taken to find dangerous drug mixes or gaps. They engage directly with the physicians caring for those members to resolve hazardous drug regimens.

HRA (health reimbursement arrangement): An employer-funded account to pay for qualifying medical expenses that employers offer to their employees. The funds may be available to pay for monthly premiums for an individually chosen health plan, depending on the type of HRA. Unused funds may carry over from year to year. See https://www.healthcare.gov/job-based-help/

Health-sharing ("health-share") program or plan: An alternative to health insurance that pools resources of a group. Members pay a monthly set amount into a collective fund that is used to help pay for other members' medical bills. Often a member must pay for services and request reimbursement from the plan. They vary in terms of membership requirements and covered expenses and conditions. Some health-sharing plans have a religious orientation and require specific beliefs for membership. Additional contributions may be requested in certain circumstances. They are not insurance but may meet the minimum requirements for coverage to avoid penalties for being uninsured that were put in place by the ACA in 2010.

Healthcare captive: A group of employers that creates a risk pool under a reinsurance policy and above the companies' risk capacity for their self-funded plans. Any excess from the captive pool can return to the captive members within the next year.

Healthcare cost and quality navigation: A vendor who has access to online cost data for hospitals and insurance companies, and assists members of a self-funded plan or aspirational health plan with navigating the system to find providers who get the best outcomes at the best price.

HEDIS (Healthcare Effectiveness Data and Information Set): A tool used by more than 90% of U.S. healthcare plans to measure

performance and aspects of care and service. See https://health.
gov/healthypeople/objectives-and-data/data-sources-and-methods/
data-sources/healthcare-effectiveness-data-and-information-set-hedis

HSA (health savings account): A tax-advantaged, U.S. govern-
ment-defined savings account that is only available to people who
have a high-deductible healthcare insurance plan. Pre-tax money is
deposited into the account and can be used for specifically defined
healthcare-related expenses without paying taxes on it. The account
is owned by individuals and goes with them if they leave the employer who provided the high-deductible insurance plan.

**Individual coverage health reimbursement arrangement
(ICHRA)**: This type of arrangement is offered to employees to
choose their own health plan and separates the employer from the
healthcare system. Employees can use the funds to purchase another
healthcare strategy outside the AH option, such as helping to pay
for a spouse's plan or purchasing a health-sharing program.

Infertility vendors: Experts for members who are struggling with infertility, to reduce the incidence of high-risk NICU (neonatal intensive care unit) care and multiple births (twins and triplets), and help
people get pregnant at lower cost, quickly, and with better outcomes.

NCQA (National Committee for Quality Assurance): A private, 501(c)(3) not-for-profit organization dedicated to improving
healthcare quality. See https://www.ncqa.org/about-ncqa/

Nuka System of Care: The original model that aspirational healthcare is based on, a relationship-based healthcare system built around
the customer by the Southcentral Foundation in Alaska for Alaska
Natives and American Indian people. Nuka is an Alaska Native
word used to mean strong, giant structures and living things.

Organ transplant assistance: A vendor who assists with both managing associated costs, such as dialysis in support of a liver transplant, and coordinating the process of getting the transplant surgery scheduled and the after-care to minimize recovery costs.

Patient Rights Advocate Organization (PatientRightsAdvocate.org): A 501(c)(3) nonprofit organization that fights for systemwide healthcare price transparency.

PBM (pharmacy benefit management company): An intermediary who coordinates and procures medications for health insurance companies, with varying degrees of transparency in operations and variable price markups on all drugs provided.

PEPM (per-employee per-month): A basis used for billing in insurance plans and specialty vendors.

PPO (preferred provider organization): A network of medical providers, including hospitals, doctors, and surgical centers, that can be accessed at a lower cost than providers that are outside this network.

Psychiatry network vendors: Vendors who provide a higher level of access to psychiatrists, and especially child psychiatrists, as these specialists are becoming more and more in demand.

Readmission prevention vendors: These vendors follow up with each patient and their caregivers immediately following discharge and make sure that the discharge plan is being followed. The result of this simple follow-up is that unnecessary readmissions to hospitals can often be prevented.

Reinsurance carriers: A reinsurance policy covers large spike claims and aggregate claims beyond a self-funded plan's willingness to risk. A good benefit consultant can guide you to a provider that meets your needs.

Secondary care: Secondary care includes specialists, imaging centers, surgical centers, and hospitals when the primary care doctor determines it is needed.

Specialty pharmacy manager: A vendor who specializes in managing the costs of high-cost specialty drugs such as biological drugs for self-funded health plans, usually in addition to a transparent standard PBM.

Surgery network: A network of surgical providers who offer bundled prices to control the cost of surgeries for your self-funded plan. The self-funded plan commonly will offer incentives for members to use these options by removing any copay or deductibles, if they go to one of these providers.

Telemedicine and teletherapy: These services allow members who choose to stay with their healthcare system-owned provider to meet many of their needs virtually, bringing down costs. These services may also be a part of APC plans.

TPA (third-party administrator): A more independent administrator for self-funded health plans, usually providing service and connection access to healthcare networks and other vendors. TPAs may not be associated with an insurance company but may offer a variety of healthcare PPO networks and also offer a wide range of additional services, including enhanced reporting.

Transparency in Coverage Rule: Passed in 2020, this rule requires hospitals to post their standard prices for all procedures online. The result is their list of prices called a *chargemaster*, which represents the price a hospital will charge in the absence of any discounts.

Transparency resources: Often these are nonprofit or not-for-profit organizations that make pricing, quality, and safety information about healthcare providers available to the public.

ENDNOTES

1. *Biggest Industries by Revenue in the U.S. in 2024.* IBISWorld Industry Reports. https://www.ibisworld.com/united-states/industry-trends/biggest-industries-by-revenue/

2. Centers for Medicare & Medicaid Services. "NHE Fact Sheet." CMS.gov. September 6, 2023. https://www.cms.gov/data-research/statistics-trends-and-reports/national-health-expenditure-data/nhe-fact-sheet

3. "Medical Informatics: Driving Data Analytics." *Health Exec*. February 16, 2022. https://healthexec.com/topics/healthcare-management/healthcare-economics/medical-informatics-driving-data-analytics

4. Froemke, Susan, Matthew Heineman, Clive Alonzo, Don Berwick, Elizabeth Blackburn, and Krystal Bracy. *Escape Fire: The Fight to Rescue American Healthcare.* IMDb. October 5, 2012. https://www.imdb.com/title/tt2093109/

5. McMains, Vanessa. "Johns Hopkins study suggests medical errors are third-leading cause of death in U.S." HUB. May 3, 2016. https://hub.jhu.edu/2016/05/03/medical-errors-third-leading-cause-of-death/

6. Papanicolas, Irene, Liana R. Woskie, and Ashish K. Jha. "Health Care Spending in the United States and Other High-Income Countries." *JAMA*. March 13, 2018. https://jamanetwork.com/journals/jama/article-abstract/2674671

7. Robbins, Rebecca, and Reed Abelson. "How PBMs Are Driving up Prescription Drug Costs." *The New York Times*. June 21, 2024. https://www.nytimes.com/2024/06/21/business/prescription-drug-costs-pbm.html

8. Merrill, Ray M., and Merrill, Grant. "An evaluation of a comprehensive, incentivized worksite health promotion program with a health coaching component." *International Journal of Workplace Health Management*, Vol. 7 Iss: 2, pp. 74–88 (2014). Emerald Group Publishing Limited. Bingley, United Kingdom.

9. Abrashoff, Michael. *It's Your Ship: Management Techniques From the Best Damn Ship in the Navy*. Grand Central Publishing (2012).

10. Kelly, Matthew. *The Dream Manager: The Secret to Attracting, Engaging, and Retaining Talent*. Hyperion (2007).

11. Burg, Bob, and Mann, John David. *The Go-Giver: A Little Story About a Powerful Business Idea*. Portfolio (2015).

12. Centers for Medicare & Medicaid Services. "Transparency in Coverage Final Rule Fact Sheet." CMS.gov. October 29, 2020. https://www.cms.gov/newsroom/fact-sheets/transparency-coverage-final-rule-fact-sheet-cms-9915-f

13. "Fact Sheet: Reference-Based Pricing." American Hospital Association. https://www.aha.org/fact-sheets/2021-06-08-fact-sheet-reference-based-pricing

RECOMMENDED READING

The Innovator's Prescription by Clayton M. Christensen

America's Bitter Pill by Steven Brill

Never Pay the First Bill by Marshall Allen

The Price We Pay by Marty Makary, M.D.

The Company That Solved Health Care by John Torinus Jr.

Healthcare Beyond Reform by Joe Flower

The Future of Health-Care Delivery by Stephen C. Schimpff, M.D.

ACKNOWLEDGMENTS

I'd like to thank the Southcentral Foundation for their education, support, and partnership in sharing the aspirational healthcare model so that more people can experience a better healthcare system. This team has accomplished truly amazing things through their Nuka System of Care.

To my team at Orriant, thank you for your passion for providing innovative healthcare solutions and for the people we work with every day. The work you do helps transform lives.

And thank you to the team at Aloha Publishing, including Maryanna Young, Heather Goetter, and Megan Terry, for their help in bringing this book from idea to print.

HEALTHCARE INNOVATION WARRIORS

There is an army of healthcare innovation warriors across the country dedicating their careers to making healthcare more customer-centric. I would like to acknowledge just a few of them.

For more information on the following names, visit:
http://MakeHealthcareWorkForYou.com

PHYSICIANS

Bill Bestermann, M.D.

Bill Hennessey, M.D.

Cristin Dickerson, M.D.

Janice Johnston, M.D.

Firouz Daneshgari, M.D.,
   MBA, FPMRS, FACS

G. Keith Smith, M.D.

Jerry Beinhauer, M.D.

Joseph Shen, M.D.

K. Andrew Crighton, M.D.

Kaylan A. Baban, M.D., MPH

Lisa M. Behnke, M.D., MHA,
   BSN

Mark Tomasulo, D.O.

Mary Tipton, M.D.

Michael D. Parkinson, M.D.,
   MPH, FACPM

Michael Jennings, M.D.

Owen Scott Muir, M.D.,
   DFAACAP

Paula Muto, M.D., FACS

Ron Stout, M.D., MPH

Soujanya (Chinni) Pulluru,
   M.D.

Stephen Schimpff, M.D.,
   MACP

Steven F. Schutzer, M.D.

Tony Dale, M.D.

INNOVATION LEADERS CREATING SIGNIFICANT IMPACT NATIONALLY

Allison Johnson

Bill Lacy

Brian Klepper, Ph.D.

Cynthia A. Fisher

Dave Chase

Dr. David Berg

E. Heidi Cottle

Jessica Brooks-Woods

Lee Lewis

Marilyn Bartlett

Nelson Griswold

Stacey Richter

Vidar Jorgensen

Wendell Potter

EMPLOYER REPRESENTATIVES LEADING THE CHANGE

Dan Ludwig

Daron Jones

Ginger Miller

John Keller

John Torinus Jr.

Kevin Clegg

Rae Barton

Stephanie M. Koch, SPHR,
    SHRM-SCP, CHVA

INNOVATIVE BENEFIT ADVISORS

Aaron Witwer, M.S.

Alan Wang

Bill L. Andersen

Bryce Heinbaugh

Colby Denton

Cristy Gupton

David Contorno, CAA

Dennis J. Walker

Donovan Pyle

Eric S. Avrumson, CEBS®,
    ChHC®, CAA

Frank M. Stichter

Jonathan Harris

Kevin Brown

Louis Bernardi

Mark Holland

Michael Juergens

Nathan Ballash, CAA

Nicholas L. Manion,
    Pharm.D., R.Ph., M.S.

Scott Haas

Scott S. Ferrin, CAA

Steve Nielsen, MHA, FACHE,
    RHU

INNOVATIVE POINT SOLUTION PROVIDERS

Al Lewis

Angie Taylor

Betsy Foster

Bibb Beale

Brad Butler

Brent Hale

Brian Garcia

Casey Billington

Chad Gray

David Silverstein

Don Sanford

Doug Burgoyne

Eric Krieg

Guy Benjamin

Jack G. London, D.D.

Jamie Greenleaf

Jay Hoffman

Joan Ziegler

Jordan Taradash

Joyce Canning

Kimberlee Langford, BSN,
    R.N., CCM, CRMT, CPC

Korb Matosich

Kristin Begley, Pharm.D.

Lee Jacobson

Lucien Morin

Mark Royal

Mark Testa, D.C., MHA

Matthew VanderKooi

Michael Hennesey

Nicole Bell

Nicole Williams

Pramod John

Robert W. Edmonds III

Robin Foust

Sally Pace

Spring Lane, MSN, FNP-C

Terry Killilea, Pharm.D.

Thompson Aderinkomi, M.S.,
    MBA

LEGAL ADVISORS

Chris Deacon

D. Douglas Aldeen, Esq.

Julie Selesnick

CEO CONSULTANTS/COACHES

Bob Hilke

Jeff Ellington

Josh Berlin

Kimberly White

Marlin Woods

INDIVIDUALS AND REPRESENTATIVES OF ORGANIZATIONS DRIVING CHANGE IN HEALTHCARE

Andrea Werner

Darren Fogarty

Donna Grande

Eric Vanderhoef

Eric Weaver, MHA, DHA

Garry Welch, Ph.D.

Jay Kempton

Jeff Hogan

Jeff Lawhead

Jennifer (Forbes) Tomasulo

Jim Purcell

John Hoben

Joni Bowen

Karen Moseley

Matt Ohrt

Nancy Spangler, Ph.D.

Paige Polakow

Patrick Blackaller

Dr. Ronke Komolafe

Roxanne (Ramoutar)
    Derhodge, B.Sc., M.Sc., R.P.

Trenton Olson

Disclaimer: In the event the reader of this book should seek a referral to any service provider referenced in this book, the person accessing the resource or provider is solely responsible for assessing the knowledge, skill, or capabilities of such provider. Neither the author, publisher, nor Orriant, Inc. are responsible for the quality, integrity, performance, or any other aspect of any services ultimately provided by such provider or any damages, consequential or incidental, arising from use of such provider.

ABOUT THE AUTHOR

Darrell T. Moon is a healthcare innovator and the founder of Orriant, focused on helping people build better relationships with healthcare. With a background as a hospital administrator, his insider knowledge exposed the root causes of many U.S. healthcare issues, from poor patient outcomes to the inefficiencies of the traditional system.

After managing 10 hospitals, Darrell developed solutions such as partnering with insurers for health coaching and founding Aspirational Healthcare, BLLC, which helps employers cut healthcare costs in half while improving employee benefits. Inspired by the Nuka System of Care, which is widely considered one of the best healthcare systems in the world, he helps companies adopt similar strategies, reducing costs and improving employee retention. His latest innovation, White Glove Healthcare, offers personalized concierge services. His goal is to create a world where people envision healthcare as a partner to help them do what they want to do.

Darrell is also a consultant, speaker, and *Forbes* Leadership Contributor, with articles featured in *Bloomberg, Business Insider*, and more. He is a top speaker to CEOs through the world's largest CEO coaching organization, Vistage. He holds degrees in finance and health administration from Brigham Young University and lives in Utah. Darrell and his wife, Laurie, have eight adult children.

DarrellMoon.com

ABOUT ORRIANT

Orriant offers what we call Premier Alignment Consulting to make your transition to aspirational healthcare easy. We walk you through every step of the process. We'll help you define your business objectives, build the monitor systems, and keep track of them. We'll help you create alignment and bring in brokers who are willing to sign a fee-based contract.

We have a variety of products to help companies of various sizes customize their healthcare offerings. For small companies, we can help you build your plan based on the four defined contribution categories. And for large employers, we offer a self-funded plan with almost every element you need covered under a single contract, the Super Plan.

Every one of Orriant's products is made to fulfill the meaning of our name, Orriant—to rise up and be happy—whether that's our corporate coaching program, corporate wellness, Aspirational Healthcare, or White Glove Healthcare. We do it through coaching, clinical care coordination, and consulting.

Orriant is here to help you do what you want to do. Rise up and embrace your journey to become the best you can be. Being healthy is about being able to do what you want to do.

The following Orriant companies and subsidiaries provide services that can be customized and combined based on your needs:

- White Glove Healthcare: Orriant's healthcare concierge services provide customer service for your self-funded health plan, with personalized assistance for navigating healthcare and meeting life aspirations.

- Aspirational Healthcare, BLLC: A wholly owned subsidiary of Orriant, Aspirational Healthcare provides services to help organizations achieve the aspirational model of healthcare based on the Nuka System of Care's principles.

- Resilience Pro: Proactive mental health services that reach out to those undergoing emotional, social, physical, behavioral, medical, and financial challenges.

- Corporate Wellness: A corporate wellness program that is focused on helping individuals reach their goals and improving population health.

- Premier Alignment Consulting (PremierAlignment.com): A CEO consulting service offered to companies big or small.

- Personal Success Coaching: Coaching integrated into primary care that helps customers reach the best possible outcomes in life.

- 1% Solution: Care management for those who regularly access healthcare to meet their social and emotional needs.

- Orriant Life: A subscription-based advanced primary care and coaching service for families. If you are considering offering subscription-based advanced primary care to only those members who want it, Orriant Life is a good option that allows individual families to sign up for both primary care and coaching together.

Orriant started out as just a corporate wellness program, and we've expanded to help everybody rise up, including individuals, families, the healthcare system, and employers. We want to help you live better. We help individuals and families rise up to reach their aspirations. We help employers rise up in how they buy healthcare. And we help the entire healthcare system rise up to be more customer-centric.

As an employer, you can combine any of Orriant's services to fit your needs. We can cover a large part of your customized healthcare plan while consulting with you on how to build your plan to meet your objectives for purchasing healthcare.

orriant

www.ingramcontent.com/pod-product-compliance
Lightning Source LLC
Chambersburg PA
CBHW030507210326
41597CB00013B/822